MATTING MOUNTING AND FRAMING ART

MATTING MOUNTING AND FRAMING ART

Max Hyder

Illustrated by Paul LaPlaca

WATSON-GUPTILL PUBLICATIONS/NEW YORK

ACKNOWLEDGMENTS

I would like to express my special thanks to the two young men who helped so much with the creation of this book; without their assistance it would not have been possible. They are my friends and former students, Paul LaPlaca, who made the photographs and the drawings to illustrate the book, and Wlodek Koss, who patiently served as model and made many of the mats and frames that appear in these pages.

The photographs that appear on pages 14, 32, 69, and 109 are copyrighted by the Koss family painters. They are used with their kind permission.

Copyright © 1986 by Max Hyder

First published 1986 in New York by Watson-Guptill Publications, a division of Billboard Publications, Inc., 1515 Broadway, New York, N.Y. 10036

Library of Congress Cataloging-in-Publication Data

Hyder, Max
  Matting, mounting, and framing art.

  Includes index.
  1. Mat cutting (Pictures)   2. Pictures—Trimming, mounting, etc.   3. Picture frames and framing.
  I. Title.
  N8550.H88   1986   749′.7   86-5534
  ISBN 0-8230-3027-X

Distributed in the United Kingdom by Phaidon Press Ltd., Littlegate House, St. Ebbe's St., Oxford

Manufactured in U.S.A.

First Printing, 1986
5 6 7 8 9 10/97 96 95 94 93 92

CONTENTS

With deep appreciation to B, without whose encouragement,
untiring dedication, and assistance
this book would have never come about.

Antique French lithograph
French mat
Gold colonial frame

1925 sepia photograph
Oval covered mat with gold bevel
Gold colonial frame

Antique French lithograph
French mat
Gold colonial frame

Nineteenth-century English hunting print
Glass mat
Gold colonial frame

Calligraphy: "Song of Solomon"
Silk-covered mat with gold bevel
Silver gilt "J" molding frame

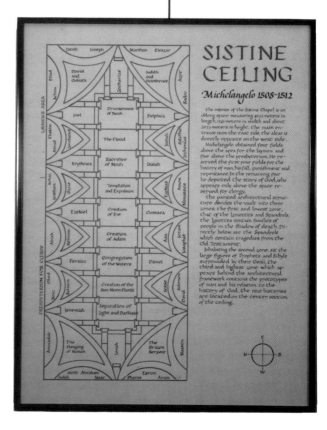

Calligraphy: map of Sistine Ceiling
Black section frame

Soy sauce can mounted on red velvet
Double shadow box frame:
Gold pyramid molding frame inside
Black O'Keeffe molding frame

Beer can mounted
on white linen

Single shadow box frame
with separator strips

Aluminum leaf box-style frame

Mixed media, *Annunciation*, by Rex Clawson
White linen mat
Mat-style frame decorated by artist

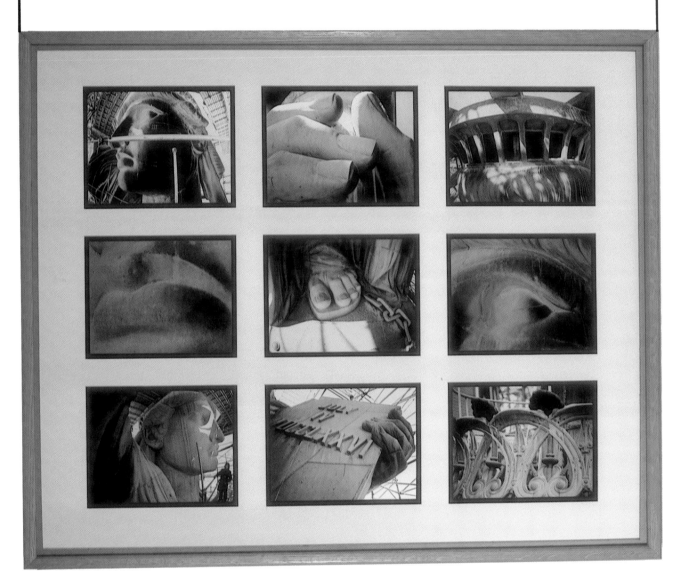

Nine color photographs by Jerzy Koss

Multiple double mat

Oak box-style frame

Pencil drawing by Reuben Kadish
Drop-on museum board backing with tan mat
Cherry "J" molding frame

Watercolor by Ferdinand Petrie
Double mat
Driftwood double-bevel frame

INTRODUCTION

There have been so many books written on every conceivable subject that it may seem a bit audacious to go right ahead and write another one. An old Chinese proverb states, "Of the making of many books there is no end." And after a little consideration and some hesitation, I too have set my hand to writing. I suppose one always secretly thinks that what he has to say may in some way be a new contribution, or at least may give a new slant, to what has probably already been said. In the writing of this book I have tried to give you the benefit of my long experience. To what extent I have been able to achieve this, only time and your own experience will tell. I have tried to make suggestions, rather than lay down rigid rules. When on occasion a student of mine tells me that he or she has found a better method than the one I use, I am so glad and not at all surprised. So whenever I tell you to use a particular material or to proceed in a special way, I hope that you will understand that this is merely the way that I have found gives best results; it certainly is not the only path! Tools and materials and methods can always vary; what is important is the result. If you find useful a tool that I have not even mentioned that's a plus and a tribute to your resourcefulness.

Many things discussed are really a matter of taste, and there is no disputing taste. If you find yourself in disagreement with me on matters of color of mats or suitability of frames this is certainly no surprise; but incorrect measurements or sloppy workmanship are not matters of opinion. A bad joint is a bad joint. I have suggested good work habits and correct procedures in as many areas as I could.

This book has been conceived and written for the serious amateur who desires to work within the limits of his or her own studio without the need for expensive equipment. The operations that I speak of in simple terms are also accomplished much more rapidly on the commercial level with the use of complex machines and techniques. I am hoping that the reader of this book will want to learn to do by hand the same things that are ordinarily done by machines, and

will want to be able to look at the results with the eye of a craftsman rather than with the eye of a consumer that demands the slick perfection of industrial products. I, too, am searching for perfection; but it is not of that sort. I look at matting and framing as I look at any other craft; I like to see the touch of the human hand. This point of view does not suggest that you should be sloppy, it just says that you shouldn't be concerned if your corners don't align exactly or if the toning of your gold leafing is not absolutely uniform. Your painted frames do not have to look like sleek refrigerators or automobiles. There is an appropriate level of perfection for everything.

Probably the most important consideration is the matter of style. By this I do not mean "fashion"; I mean that quality which sets one individual apart from another as in the style of a Rubens or a Van Gogh. I mean developing your own way of doing things so that your work will bear your signature in the way it looks, so that those seeing it will recognize it as yours. As you repeatedly perform the various operations involved in matting and framing and exercise your taste in the selection of colors and textures, you will begin to settle into patterns of repeated combinations that have pleased you until eventually your work takes on an identity of its own.

While writing this book, I have kept in mind that readers come from a wide cross-section of experience. Some of you will be more familiar with the terms and processes discussed here, while others of you will need more clarification. In the hope that this book not be too simple for those with previous experience, and yet offer sufficient explanation for the neophyte, I have begun each section with an overview of the entire procedure. This general discussion establishes the subject matter and deals in depth with the details of the process. This material is followed by a step-by-step demonstration complete with detailed captions. Although by themselves these captions contain everything you will need to know to follow the demonstration, I think that reading the initial general text will provide a more comprehensive look at the procedure to follow.

Good luck with your projects,
Max Hyder
New York City, 1986

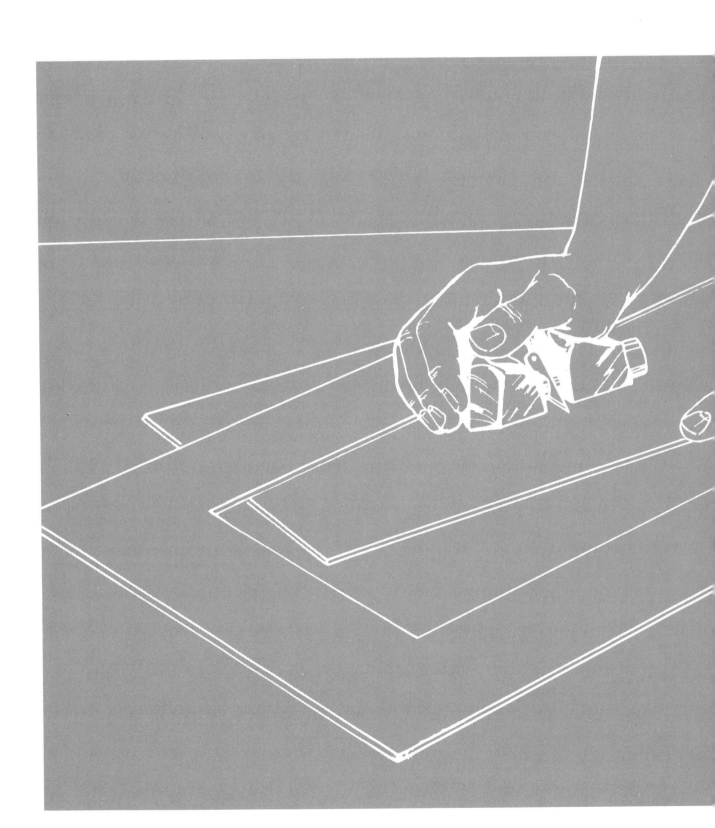

PART ONE

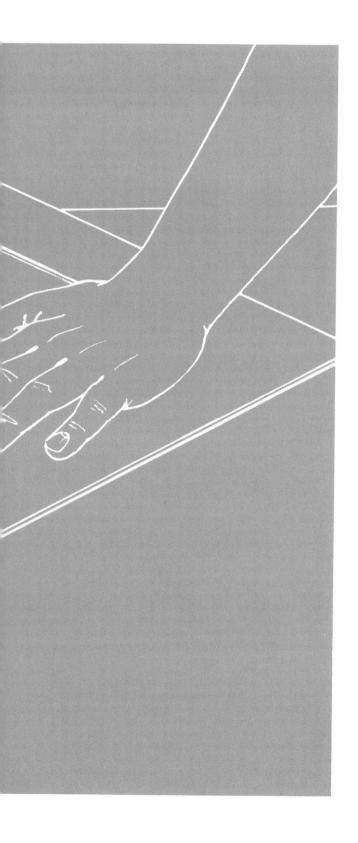

MATTING

Of all the devices used in the enhancement and presentation of art, the mat is without doubt the most common and the most diverse. The earliest picture frames were in effect mats. The outer border of the painting panel of a Byzantine icon, for example, was left undecorated so that the painting was surrounded by neutral space. This area was often slightly raised, affording some protection for the painted surface. This flat, or mat-style, frame is still in use today. The making of mat-style frames is discussed in Part Two.

Areas of empty space surrounding a work of art generally add to the impact of the piece. If a piece is very large, it often will not benefit from having neutral space around it, but, almost invariably, small and moderate-size works of art need some kind of mat. When framing drawings, photographs, prints, or other works on paper, the preferred matting material is paperboard or card-board. Paintings on canvas or panels usually have wooden inserts, or liners, instead of mats. In the area of covered mats there is a fine line between what might, strictly speaking, be called a "mat" and what could be considered a liner or an insert. In any case, the function of mats and liners is the same. Of the major types of mats, the folder mat is the most basic paperboard mat. Folder mats are used, with or without frames, for most works on paper. The folder mat consists of an overmat, usually with a cut window, and a backing piece, which is hinged with paper or cloth to the overmat. The artwork is sandwiched between overmat and backing piece, and is usually attached to the backing with small linen tape hinges or peelable paper hinges. In some cases the work may need to be mounted, that is, glued or otherwise attached, to the backing piece.

Deciding to use a cut mat—a mat with a window—or to simply lay the work against a background—to achieve the effect of a mat—depends on a number of things. When framing an etching, engraving, lithograph, drawing, water-color, or other type of artwork on paper, the cut mat is usually preferable. An exception might be made if the paper on which the work is done has an interesting edge.

A contemporary woodcut printed on rice paper with frayed edges would, for example, look good against, perhaps, a linen-covered board. This treatment is called drop-on, and is often applied when there is a natural deckle or a torn imitation. The drop-on is usually held in place by two small linen tape hinges attached to the underside of the upper corners. The floating effect produced by drop-on is often enhanced by adding a cut mat; the window of the mat exposes a portion of the backing piece. It is not wise to use this drop-on technique with a fabric-covered board. In most cases, white matboard is best for both mat and backing, but occasionally a colored board can be used effectively.

The color of the mat is most important. Usually white or off-white mats work best. Occasionally black or gray works well. Real colors are almost always wrong. Colored mats are in common use; they are often used in elaborate ways to produce highly decorative effects. This is fine if you are displaying the mat, but a colored mat won't work if what you want to display is art.

Framers are frequently asked by interior designers to create arrangements or groupings of several pictures that will be tied to a color scheme by the effective use of matting. I remember doing such an arrangement in which there were nine pictures of varying shape and size—all with wide mats covered with MacDonald plaid. The same fabric was used for the draperies, the upholstery of the couch, and two chairs. I have no memory as to what the pictures were like; but I certainly remember the mats. I always try to make both mats and frames secondary to the work being framed. Quiet tones in mats and subdued finished in frames are invariably pleasing. When matting photographs, it is best to limit the mat choice to white, off-white, gray, or black. The frames should be narrow, the mats wide. The frame should be silver, gray, black, or white. Incidentally, the aluminum section frames now so widely available are particularly good for photographs.

I tend to avoid natural wood and gold effects when working with photographs. I have used these effects, and even some very ornamental moldings, when framing old or sepia-toned or hand-colored photographs. Such an example is included in the oval mat section. There, to enhance an old brown-toned photograph, I used a moleskin mat with a gold bevel. The photograph was taken in a time when photography was more or less in competition with painting. When photography was young, photographers tried to make pictures that would rival drawings or pastel sketches. Today, we have a different consciousness about photography, and contemporary photographs require treatment that does not echo the styles used for the framing of drawings and paintings. In most cases, it is best to keep the style simple; the closer to a "no-frame" effect the better.

Sometimes the mat effect is achieved by simply mounting the photograph on matboard. This practice has been popularized by the widespread use of the dry-mount process. Since dry mounting makes it possible to precisely control the positioning of the photograph, it is possible to establish even borders. Although dry-mount materials are available for use with ordinary hand irons, this process is best done with a dry-mount press. (See the section on mounting, (pages 126 to 135), and refer also to the discussion of spacers (pages 88 to 89) in the framing section.) If you do not wish to mount your photograph, a cut mat with window will work well. Photographs benefit from the drop-on method. Since the paper is emulsion-coated on only one side, photographs have a tendency to curl.

The selection of a correct neutral shade for a mat can be a problem. There are certain established board colors that are accepted standards for the industry. The Bainbridge matboard number 128 (off-white) is always a safe choice. It goes with everything. Bainbridge brilliant white is usually a bit startling. It works well if you are seeking a crisp effect. If you are matting a black ink line drawing done on a very white paper, Bainbridge brilliant white may be perfect; you might even color the bevel with India ink.

As a general rule, try to make the mat tone

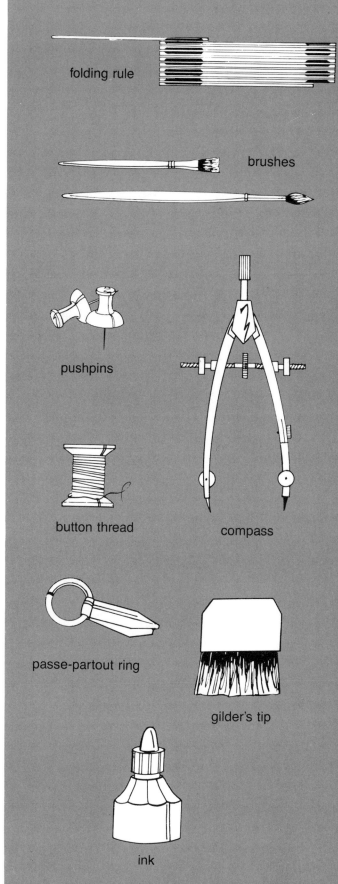

folding rule

brushes

pushpins

button thread

compass

passe-partout ring

gilder's tip

ink

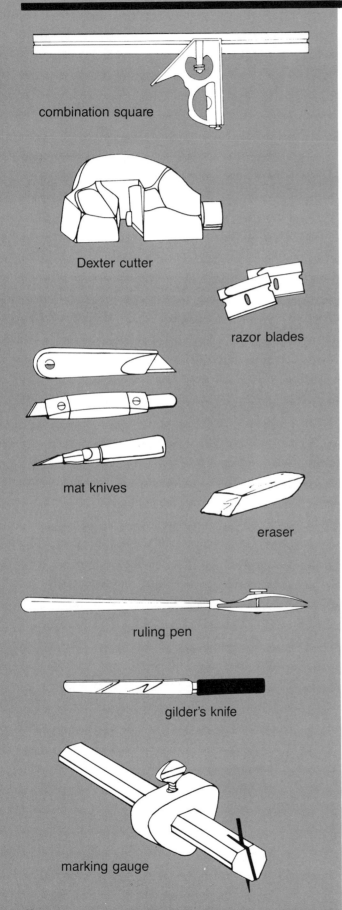

combination square

Dexter cutter

razor blades

mat knives

eraser

ruling pen

gilder's knife

marking gauge

darker than the tone of the paper of the drawing. If you are framing an etching, lithograph, or other "toned-in" kind of work, don't let the mat color exceed the highest value in the artwork. Make the mat darker and you will inevitably enhance the piece. To apply this rule, it may sometimes be necessary to use a mat in the cream or even the tan range. Because of the quality of paper, prints that are almost brown in tone may require tan or brown matting.

Occasionally the need arises for rather large mats. Normal matboard is 30″ × 40″ (76.2 × 101.6 cm) or 32″ × 40″ (81.2 × 101.6 cm), although it is also available in 40″ × 60″ (101.6 × 86.2 cm) and even 48″ × 72″ (131.9 × 183 cm). Usually it is best to use these larger mats in double-thickness. These boards are expensive and are not always available. As a substitute, I sometimes use a builder's cardboard known as Upson board. This board, or something similar, is available in most lumberyards and building supply stores. It comes in 4′ × 8′ (1.2 × 2.42 m) sheets, and is moderately priced. The boards are available in a number of thicknesses, but the most commonly available ones are the ⅛″ (.32 cm) and the ³⁄₁₆″ (.48 cm); the latter size is more useful. There is ¼″ (.64 cm) also, but it is more difficult to cut for bevels. Upson board, although not archival, is satisfactory for many needs. When doing museum-quality work you should, of course, use higher-quality board. Upson board does serve well, however, as a mounting board, and nice deep bevels can be made when the board is used as an undermat. The board also provides extra distance between glass and art when used for a covered mat; and it is an excellent support for linen or other fabric when used as background for a drop-on.

If thickness is not a requirement, rag papers, two-ply museum-board, or two-ply bristol are often adequate matting materials. Mats made from these materials are not cut with bevels. Foam-core and corrugated cardboard do not qualify as matting materials. They can be useful as backing when framing.

THE FOLDER MAT

The folder mat is the basic mat. The material used to make it is normal matboard; when more archival considerations are in order, museum-board or other high-rag content paperboards are often used. For most work the standard matboards available in art supply stores are sufficient. As mentioned earlier, they normally come in 30″ × 40″ (76.2 × 101.6 cm) or 32″ × 40″ (81.2 × 101.6 cm) sheets. The 32″ size allows for the cutting of four 16″ × 20″ (40.6 × 50.8 cm) mats, which is by far the most commonly used size.

The folder mat requires two pieces of board of the same size. For the sake of economy the backing piece is sometimes made of a less expensive type of board such as chipboard (gray tablet backing) or posterboard. If you use cheaper backings you might consider using a backing or barrier sheet of higher-quality paper between the artwork and the backing piece. There are special barrier papers available with a neutral pH and, in some cases, 100 percent rag.

There are many ways to cut mats. Since all of the professional cutting machines come with their own set of instructions, I am going to assume that you are interested in learning to do the job without special devices. Although an unskilled person can cut a perfect mat with a professional cutter, the degree of skill required to cut an acceptable mat by hand can be learned with just a few sessions of practice. I am including in the expression "by hand" the several hand-held cutters that are used instead of a knife, such as the Dexter, the Chartpack, and the X-Acto. These inexpensive blade holders enable you to maintain a constant bevel angle, thus requiring less skill than a knife does.

If there's a secret to good cutting, it's a good knife. The Stanley utility knife with changeable blades is a sturdy knife and each blade has two usable ends. There are many others; but I would avoid those that retract into the handle, because they have a tendency to slip back into the handle while you are cutting. Other knives like those in which the blade extends beyond the handle and can be hand-sharpened on a whetstone are also good. While sharpening

takes some time, this type of knife is economical and you get a newly sharpened edge every time. I used one of these hand-sharpened matknives daily for eight years—and never changed the blade. Even if you decide to cut your mats with one of the blade holder blocks like the Dexter, you will still need a good sharp knife to cut the mat's outside dimensions.

A good straight-edge is another tool that is really necessary for good cutting. If you are using one of the block-type cutters, you can do very well with an inexpensive metal ruler. (I would suggest one that is at least 4′ [1.22 m] long.) However, if you are using a knife, it's preferable to go for a straight-edge made from steel and that comes with a beveled edge. (The beveled edge allows you to place the straight-edge closer to the line.) These beveled straight-edges are expensive and you can get by with the metal alloy-type ruler; but eventually the metal alloy edge will be knicked by the knife.

You will need a dead-end ruler. I use a standard folding rule the 6′ (1.8 m) type is sufficient. The extendable-type ruler used for inside measurement is helpful but not necessary, although if you are fitting mats into pre-existing frames, you may find it helpful.

The only other tool I will suggest, other than a number 2 pencil, is hardly a "tool" at all. It is a hardwood bar of a convenient dimension—the marking block. It must be straight and "square." If you do not have the means to make one, a friendly cabinetmaker should be able to produce it for you. The one shown here is made of poplar wood. Rock-maple is heavier, but any good hardwood will do.

The marking block should be "jointed," that is, made straight on a jointer and cut to parallel dimension on the table saw. This will give you a point of true reference for abutting pieces of board or the end of your ruler. The block need only be a rectangular bar; I have added "V" grooves along the sides to make it easier to handle. It should be 3″ or 4″ (7.6 or 10 cm) wide and about 30″ (76.2 cm) long. The thickness is arbitrary, as is the width; all you are seeking is a good, solid, and straight point of reference.

When cutting out your mat, you will need a place to work. A regular-size table is fine or a drawing table turned flat will also work. The ideal table height is around 42″ (106.6 cm) high, the approximate (depending on your height) level at which you can cut comfortably without bending over.

To demonstrate the laying out and cutting of the basic mat, I have chosen a traditional Japanese woodcut. This print, because it is a woodcut, has a self-limiting edge, which is appropriate to expose. Most etchings, lithographs, and other prints fall into this category, where the edge of the art and a certain amount of border area determines more or less the size of the "window" or opening in the mat. It is the usual practice for the artist to sign and number the print below and outside the area of the image. This means that the mat opening should include a certain amount of the paper outside the actual image. The actual amount, however, needs to be judged visually. In many cases I have found that approximately ⅜″ (1 cm) beyond the edge of the art is a good border size, but in some situations, a larger border is called for.

Determining the window area for a drawing or other work of art that does not have a self-limiting edge will, of course, be more arbitrary. In drawing, for instance, some artists work within the parameters of the given space. I mean they consider the edges of the paper on which they are drawing and compose accordingly, often filling the page to its edges.

THE FOLDER MAT

In such cases it becomes difficult to overlap any part of the page with the mat. Other artists center on the drawing itself and place it randomly on the paper, in which case it is the job of the framer to decide what space should be left around it by measuring for an opening in the mat that will not crowd the subject but at the same time will eliminate unnecessary background. When a satisfactory dimension has been determined, write it down.

The next step is to determine the width of mat. This is what makes or breaks the success of the matted piece. Pieces that you don't intend to frame, such as pieces shown in a portfolio, should be generously matted. Many times these pieces are matted to a standard size for the sake of the portfolio. On the other hand, if you are matting for framing, I would suggest a different approach. Although there really is no "correct" width for matting, the usual mat width for framed pieces is 3″ to 4″ (7.6 to 10 cm). This width works well for most pieces of art.

For vertical subjects, I prefer to leave a wider margin at the bottom because of a visual perception problem that we call "visual drop," which tells our eyes that the bottom border is smaller than the top even though it is the same. For this reason it has become customary to enlarge the lower border, although the Japanese have exploited this visual trick to great advantage. When mounting their scroll paintings, they make the upper borders five times wider than the lower, thereby creating a sense of floating in space. This extreme challenge to the eye liberates us from making the decision about whether the border is "even." Incidentally, in these cases the side borders are usually even and comparatively narrow.

In Western matting the visual drop phenomenon is not often exploited; when it is, it is most often in the reverse. We sometimes mat photographs with very wide bottoms. I once framed a show of photographs in which all the mats were the same 16″ × 20″ (40.6 × 50.8 cm) format. These photographs were small and "floated" high on the vertical mats. The effect was very successful, but it did not give the floating effect that I have seen in the wide top mounting of oriental art.

Even though there are really no rules for determining mat widths, I will assume that vertical mats generally have a 3″ × 3½″ (7.62 × 8.89 cm) format. Horizontal mats do not seem to cause so much difficulty. In these cases, I either allow for ¼″ (.64 cm) extra at the bottom or nothing at all. Only experience can tell you when you need extra space and what width mat will be most effective. In the case of the woodcut shown here, I feel that 2½″ (6.35 cm) at the top and sides and 2¾″ (6.99 cm) at the bottom are sufficient since part of the paper will be exposed around the image, which effectively adds to the width of the mat. The window size of 10⅛″ × 14¾″ (25.7 × 37.5 cm) allows for a nicely balanced border. When you add the mat widths to the border widths, it produces a finished mat size of 15⅛″ × 20″ (38.4 × 50.8 cm).

Cut two pieces of matboard to the finished mat size. For this mat I have chosen Bainbridge 128 (off white), which comes in 32″ × 40″ (81.2 × 101.6 cm). Begin by marking the board at the 20″ (50.8 cm) point by butting the edge of the board against the marking block; then, using the folding rule, mark dots at three points across the board. It is best to make three dots rather than two because when you align the straight-edge, the three points will tend to compensate for error. Then, placing a scrap strip of board under the area to protect the work surface from the knife, position the straight-edge and cut the board in half with a utility knife. It helps in this operation to place a weight, such as a large book, a brick, or an iron, on the straight-edge to prevent it from slipping. Clamping should not be necessary.

Make your cut in two strokes. (I have found it helpful to place a strip of masking tape on the bottom side of the straight-edge; it acts as a permanent non-skid device.) The first pass with the knife should only score the surface; the second will follow in the cut and go all the way through. Heavier boards may require up to six passes. Then turn the half-sheet of matboard in the other direction against the marking block and mark the three points at 15⅛″ (38.42 cm). Cut this piece, then mark and cut the other one.

The next step is called the "layout." A layout is done in order to show the position and size of the window. There are two ways of doing this depending on the method you use to cut the mat. If you are cutting with a hand-held knife, the drawing is done on the front. (Be careful not to go past the corners.) The lines should be cut away and there should be no need to erase. An alternate method is to cut from the back using one of the block-type cutters with an angled blade. In this case the lines are drawn on the back and are deliberately crossed and extended beyond the corners. Methods for drawing the lines can be varied. One way is to butt the mat edge against the marking block and using the folding rule, mark the three guide dots. Be careful to make the border wider at the bottom. When marking on the back, some people use a standard carpenter's marking gauge. If you frequently repeat certain widths, it can be time-saving to cut strips of matboard to these widths and label them on the face. Simply lay the strip on top of the mat with the edges of both butted against the marking block and draw your pencil along the edge of the strip. These strips will hold up through many markings.

After you have marked the mat from the front, place it on a table with the line you intend to cut first closest to you and parallel to your body. Be sure you have your scrap strip of board under the cut. Then place the straight-edge a little before the line. The exact distance will depend on the angle of the knife and the thickness of the straight-edge. The knife might possibly be held at about 60° (that is, 30° off vertical); and if the straight-edge is not very thick, the distance away from the line should be about ³⁄₁₆″ (.48 cm). This position will then allow the knife to remove the line and produce an opening approximately the same size as the drawing. If you are cutting left to right, and you are right-handed, place a weight on the left end of the straight-edge. Left-handed persons usually reverse this procedure. For most cuts, a weight should be enough to keep the straight-edge from slipping. However, if the cut is very long, you may want to attach the straight-edge to the table edge with a "C" clamp.

With the blade resting against the straight-edge, the knife should be inserted about ⅛″ (.32 cm) beyond the corner. Then draw the knife firmly along stopping the cut about ⅛″ (.32 cm) past the corner. Slight over-cutting usually occurs at the corners; this is corrected somewhat by lightly burnishing the cut either with a tool or fingernail. If you have trouble accepting this effect as part of the look of a hand-cut mat, you may find that cutting from the back using one of the block-type cutters will give you more control. If the center does not drop out, it means you have not gone far enough. Use a blade to free the corners. Sometimes a slight raggedness results from using a dull blade or from not shifting the scrap strip underneath as you make each cut. Each new cut should go into a clean place on the scrap, not into an old cut. This ragged condition can often be corrected with very fine sandpaper. Sometimes simply rubbing with a clean rag is all it takes to rid the edge of fuzziness.

When cutting from the back, I use a Dexter cutter. The various brands of cutters have slightly differing features. Some cut 60° bevels; others cut any angle from straight to 45°. The blade should be inserted with the cutting edge facing forward. Check the depth by setting the cutter on the edge of a piece of matboard and inserting the tip of the blade slightly into a scrap underneath. Then, with the mat placed face down and the piece of scrap board underneath, insert the blade tip into the drawn line that is facing away from you and more or less perpendicular to your body. Bring the straight-edge up against the body of the cutter and position it parallel to the line. The blade should be ¹⁄₁₆″ (.16 cm) outside the crossing of the corner. Some like to use a T-square for this operation, but whether you use a T-square or a straight-edge, you will find it easier if you place a weight on the far end. Push the cutter steadily away from you, keeping it firmly against the straight-edge. Watch closely and end the cut ¹⁄₈″ (.16 cm) beyond the corner.

You are now ready to complete the folder mat except that in the example shown here I have chosen to color the bevel, so this operation should be completed before hinging the mat to the backing. The bevel acts as a separate element between mat and artwork. It accents in a dramatic way much like a line on the mat but is easier to make. (See the section on French mats if you are interested in making decorative lines on the mat.)

There are several ways to make the colored bevel. The technique shown here is not difficult and is reasonably fast. Colored drawing inks (red and brown) have been mixed in a small container. (Red seems to add spark to this rather cool gray-blue picture, but I thought the pure red a bit too bright so I added a little brown to subdue it.) Using a pointed sable watercolor brush, apply the ink to the bevel as shown, reaching from the underside of the mat so as to give you more control. The cut edge acts somewhat like a blotter and helps you to control the flow. Use the side of the brush and not the tip. If there are small over-runs on the face of the mat, they can be removed when dry by scraping with a razor-blade. Remember to scrape very gently so as not to disturb the surface paper of the matboard.

Watercolors also work very well for coloring the bevel; they are applied in the same way as ink. Some people prefer pastels; the square variety works best. When working with pastels, you should spray the bevel first with workable fixative. When this is dry, color the bevel with pastel from the underside, and clean off any smudging with a white plastic eraser. Finish by sealing with clear spray fixative.

To hinge the mat to the backing, place them next to each other with the tops touching and the mat side face down. Make hinges with pieces of tape or run one strip of tape almost all the way across the top. There are several types of tape that work well for this. Ordinary gummed white paper is satisfactory, or, if you wish a more archival type, white linen gummed tape is also good. Linen tape is available in art supply stores and has a neutral pH. Avoid the self-adhesive tapes such as masking tape or clear plastic tape. There are a few self-adhesive tapes on the market that are good for archival work; but they are usually sold only by picture framing supply houses.

When you have taped the two boards together, close the folder mat and press down on the taped end to crease the tape hinge. Be sure you have properly aligned the edges,

the last step in the making of the folder mat. Then slip the artwork into position under the window and position it for the most pleasing effect. If there is some point for measuring the artwork, such as a plate mark in an etching, you might check with a ruler to see that the borders are correct.

When you are satisfied that the position is correct, place a weight on the artwork to hold it. Then open the mat, laying the window piece face down on the table and leaving both hands free to attach the work. To attach the art, use two small linen tape hinges or pieces of book-mending tape or mulberry paper hinges, one on each side of the top. In lieu of these special materials, you can also fashion hinges from the gummed lip of an envelope or the extra gummed portions that are included in a sheet of postage stamps. These materials are at least not harmful to your artwork. *Never* use rubber cement. This material has ruined many a piece of art. It is widely used in the commercial art field because of its quick resolution; but in most of those cases the "art" is of no consequence and is intended to be thrown away after it has served its purpose.

Never use glue of any kind. Although wheat paste, mounting paste, or bookbinders polyvinyl adhesive (P.V.A.) are often used to attach the entire back of the piece to a board, if they are used in only a small spot they will cause shrinkage and pull that is not correctable. Remember, if the hinges are going to be visible because of their necessary placement at the top corners or because of the thinness of the paper, it is often a good solution to place the hinges behind a part of the image, instead of at the edge or under the clear part of the paper. By "hinge," I mean a small piece of tape or paper bridging the edge of the artwork and the backing board and pasted on the front of both. Or, it can be a folded piece stuck to the back of the art and to the front of the backing board.

For many pieces this completes the folder mat. It is now ready for presentation, for covering with acetate for use in a portfolio, or for framing. In cases where the art requires mounting, it should be done before matting and on larger board. The mounting process frequently enlarges a piece, so the measuring for the mat should not be done until after it is mounted; the board should be larger than the anticipated backing because of the difficulty of positioning the piece correctly on the mounting board. After making the mat, it may be placed on the artwork and marked so that the mounting board may be cut to the proper size.

The Japanese woodcut shown here is held in place simply by two linen tape hinges. This allows the paper to expand and contract with atmospheric changes and keeps rippling and buckling to a minimum.

Often such artwork as Japanese woodcuts, Chinese scrolls, or Tibetan tankas are framed in fake or even real bamboo frames. My feeling is that this is almost always a mistake and reflects an attitude similar to some of the early Hollywood stereotypes of subjects such as this. These subjects are usually best framed in very simple frames of the box or rounded box variety. Most of the time plain paper mats are also sufficient; but when a richer effect is desirable, such as when the piece is very fine or the setting where it will be displayed requires a more elegant touch, you might consider using something like a silk-covered mat (say natural pongee or shantung) and perhaps a gold-beveled undermat. A gold frame might also add to the effect. I have often used this type of framing on Indian or Persian miniatures.

THE FOLDER MAT

1 Using the folding rule, determine and record the window opening measurements. Add to these dimensions the width of the mat, which in this case is a 2½″ (6.35 cm) border at the top and sides and a 2¾″ (6.99 cm) at the bottom.

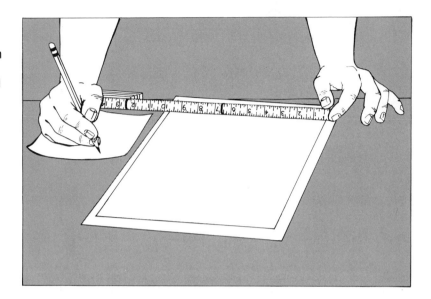

2 With both the mat edge and the folding rule abutting the marking block, mark three dots to assure the accuracy and the straightness of the cutting line.

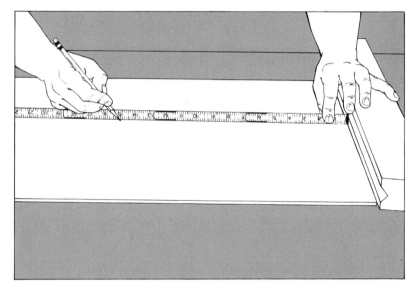

3 Using the straight-edge and utility knife, cut the matboard to size. Make sure to place a piece of scrap board under the mat to protect the table. A weight placed on the far end of the straight-edge will help keep it from slipping. Remember, it's not necessary to cut through on the first stroke; it's better (and safer) to make two or more passes using lighter pressure.

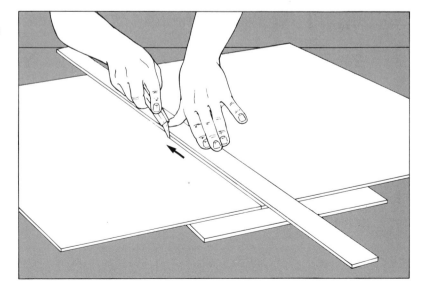

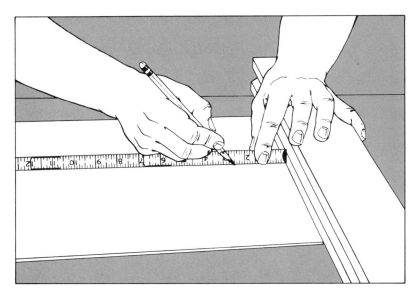

4 Abut the matboard and folding rule against the marking block. Make three dots at the proper mat width.

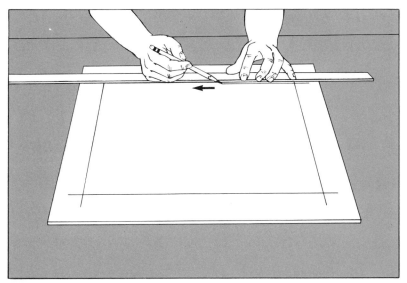

5 Using the straight-edge, draw the lines outlining the window opening, but be careful not to go beyond the corners.

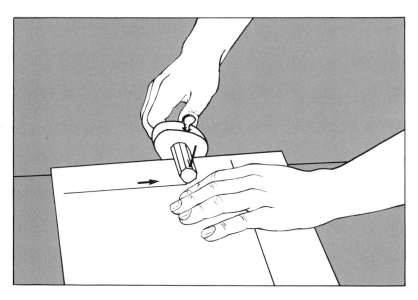

6 Mark the window from the back, using a standard carpenter's marking gauge. In this case, the cut will be made with a Dexter cutter.

7 If you are using the handheld knife, place the straight-edge a little back of the line. The distance varies according to the thickness of the straight-edge, but usually it is ⅛″ to ¼″ (.32 cm to .64 cm). Hold the knife similar to a pencil and insert it a little beyond the corner at about a 60° angle.

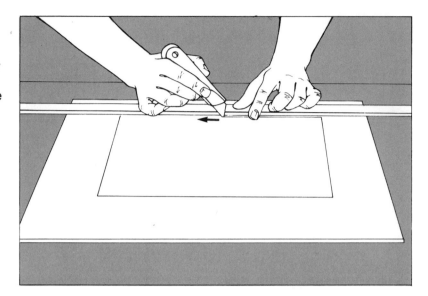

8 If the knife method proves difficult and you find you can't cut the matboard, try a Dexter or other block-style cutter. Align the straight-edge against the body of the cutter and make it parallel to the line. Make the cut by pushing down rather than by pulling along the line.

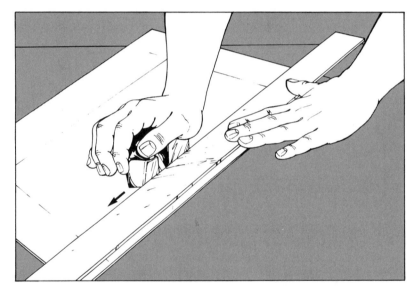

9 After all cuts have been made, the window opening should fall out easily.

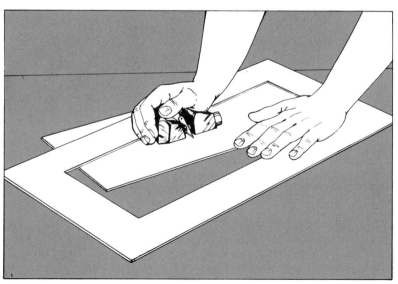

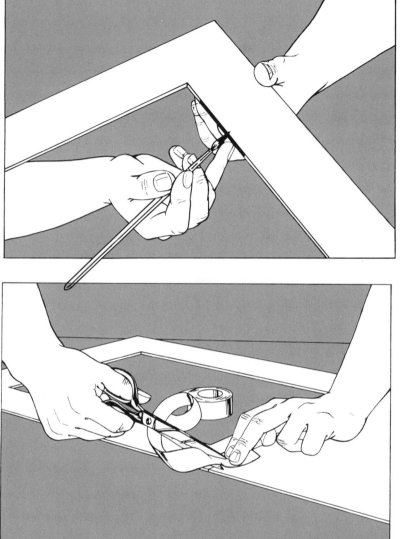

10 Hold the mat from underneath and color the bevel with red and brown drawing ink. In this position, the brush is used more from the side than from the tip. Bevels can also be colored with pastels; just spray with a workable fixative beforehand and after coloring, spray with a clear fixative.

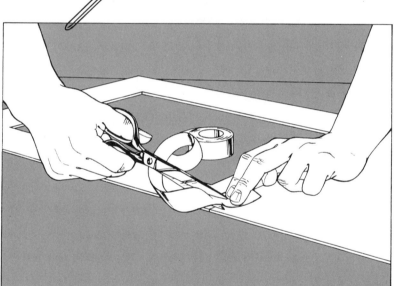

11 Cut linen tape to length to form the hinge. Gummed paper tape is also satisfactory for this purpose.

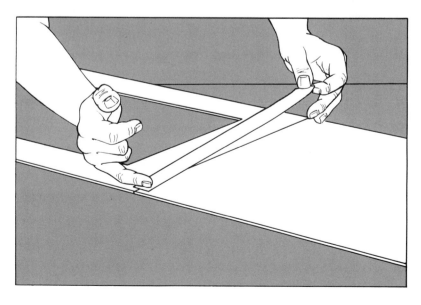

12 Join the two matboards with a hinge made of linen tape.

13 When you have taped the two boards together, close the folder mat and press down on the tape to crease the tape hinge. Make sure to properly align the edges, the last step in the making of a folder mat.

14 Position the artwork in the folder mat. If there is some point or mark for measuring the art, such as a plate mark in an etching, check with a ruler to see that the borders are even.

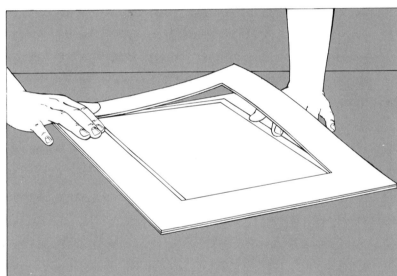

15 Attach the artwork to the backing of the mat with linen tape hinges. When enough extra paper is available, this can be done by simply overlapping the tape on the front. If the paper on which the art is done is transparent, it's usually better to place the hinge behind the art rather than underneath the white paper.

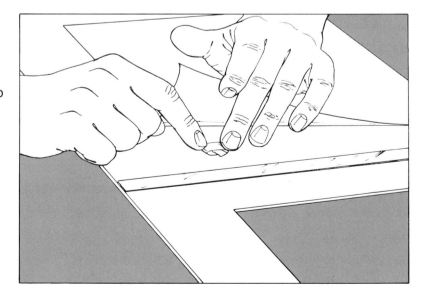

LAYERED MATS

Double and triple mats have more than one piece of matboard framing the art. These mats are used to create a more decorative bordering for the art piece and are often of contrasting color. In fact, layered matting often implies the use of color. For example, I have used red, white, and blue matboard to frame antique patriotic postcards. These pieces were very effective. However, keep in mind that when you use color in this manner you are in effect creating a new piece of art. The postcard then becomes only one of the elements in the assemblage—appropriate in some cases, but questionable when used to mat "real" pieces of art.

The layered (either double or triple) mat can be an effective design solution, however. For example, there have been times when I found it desirable to use a gray mat with a particular piece but felt that the gray should not butt up directly against the work. In these cases, I have set off the art with a ¼″ (.64 cm) border of white. This narrow white mat thus helps to establish the boundary of the art. Remember, that these proportions might be varied when framing a piece done on white paper, such as a line drawing. In that case, the mat should be exposed perhaps ³⁄₁₆″ to ¼″.

When using layered mats, the top mat should be of whatever color or tone you have decided on and should complete the total mat width. Because of the close tolerance required, layered mats are probably best cut with a mat cutter rather than a knife. If, on the other hand, you are using professional mat machines, it is quite easy to maintain the proper width variation. The set-back of the overmat should be at least ⅛″ (.32 cm); otherwise, you might as well use the colored bevel technique, which, in most cases, is what I prefer. Sometimes a wider space than ¼″ (.64 cm) is used, but beware of making the mat wider than this. The undermat gives the visual impression of a line, and we seldom read lines as wider than ¼″ (.64 cm). If you feel inclined to introduce color into the mat, you might consider the French mat, covered on pages 44 to 47.

Occasionally the need arises to frame a group of pictures in one frame, either because they form a series or are related in some other way. When this is done the multiple mat is often the most pleasing answer to the question of how best to display them. A grouping of family photographs can be made into an arrangement with each picture having its varying opening and shape. Perhaps you have a series of watercolor sketches all of a size and related in subject, so three or four of them arranged next to each other in a horizontal row might work well. I once framed such a group showing the same tree painted in each of the seasons. For this book I have chosen to frame nine photographs of the Statue of Liberty taken at close range (from the scaffolding erected to refurbish her for her hundredth birthday). The matting is not only multiple (having nine openings), but double; it shows a black undermat to add dramatic emphasis. I arrived at the layout by laying the nine 8″ × 10″ (20.3 × 25.4 cm) photographs on a full sheet 32″ × 40″ (81.2 × 101.6 cm) of off-white matboard and arranging them to a pleasing distance apart but leaving the wider margins for the outside borders. Some would argue that they should have been grouped tighter with less space between and more space around the outside. But that is a matter of taste. Some others would even insist that the spaces both between and around should have been made greater. If this were the case, it would have meant going to oversize matboard, and the glass would have gotten considerably heavier.

So multiple mats can afford an opportunity to exercise creativity. The arrangement and spacing of the openings is a primary concern and can make or break the success of the job. I have used this system to frame many things other than art; for example, postage stamps and money. In these cases I cut the openings larger than the objects and backed the mat with another piece of white matboard on which I floated the pieces. I have even matted coins in this manner (making the openings square) and military service ribbons. The use of thick boards for the top mat to create more depth to the opening almost puts us in the area of the shadow box.

LAYERED MATS

This woodcut is handsomely set off by a double mat. The narrow inner black mat serves as a border for the art, and the wider white mat makes a graceful transition to the black section frame. The black-and-white color scheme was chosen to complement the woodcut which is black ink printed on white paper.

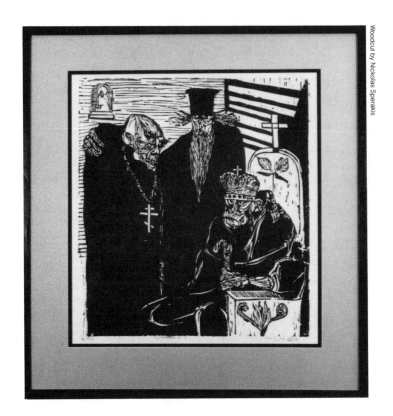

Woodcut by Nicklas Sperakis

The triple-tiered and tri-colored decorativeness of this triple mat complements the ornate architecture of the building in the photograph. The black inner mat creates a border for the photograph and also reflects the black of the frame. The middle and outer mats' cream and tan colors harmonize with the warm tones of the photograph. The rounded shape of the frame was selected to reflect the shape of the building.

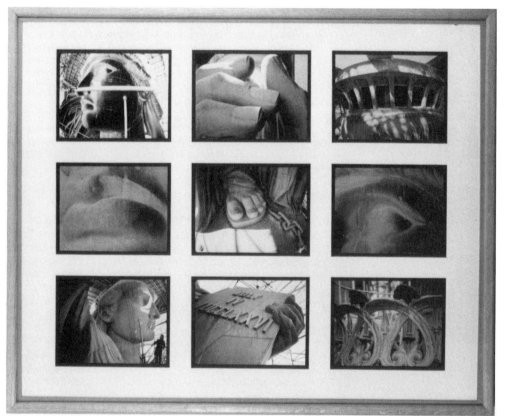

The multiple mat is a good solution for situations where related pieces of art need to be shown together. In this case, a series of photographs of the Statue of Liberty are displayed in a large mat punctuated by nine openings. Since all the photographs in this series are intended to be shown the same size, the openings in the mat are all the same size. However, in situations where the art warrants different sizes, the openings can have varied dimensions. A typical example is a display of family photographs.

A strainer, or retainer, was needed for the multiple mat in order to carry the weight of the large frame.

Screws are used to hold the strainer in place.

THE COVERED MAT

One way to enhance the effect of the mat is to give it special texture and color by covering it with various kinds of fabric. This is a little like upholstering a chair rather than leaving it plain. The problem is similar in several ways. The correct choice of fabric or other cover is essential. We have all seen unfortunate choices in upholstery materials, so if you decide to cover a mat make very sure you have chosen the correct fabric.

There are certain time-honored coverings for mats. The classic is raw silk, usually found in the form of pongee or shantung. Next to silk is linen; white is typically used but it is also found in natural tones of "wheat" or "oatmeal." Sometimes a coarser material is needed, but normally linen is as open a weave as you should use. The other widely used group of fabrics for covering mats is the velvet/velveteen range, a category that includes the moleskin used to cover the oval mat in the oval mat section. The short-napped and the so-called velveteen are best for matting purposes; "plush" or long-napped rayon velvets are much more difficult to use. Occasionally polished cotton broad-cloth will be found to be the right thing. Never use satin or taffeta or any of the thin dress materials; you can see through them to the board beneath. Many people use polyester fabrics as a substitute for silk, because silk has become very expensive. However, not all glues work on polyester, although there is a special one called "Poly-fab" that works well with synthetic fabrics.

There are two basic methods for covering mats. You can adhere the fabric to the face of the mat, then turn it face down, trim the edges, cut out the center, leaving flaps to pull over and glue down on the back. Or, you can lay the mat face down on the fabric and apply the gluing only on the back. I generally follow the first method, but if you are using a lightweight fabric or that has an open weave where the glue would seep through, perhaps the second method is best.

Using Poly-fab, Jade Adhesive, or bookbinders P.V.A. and a brush or roller, coat the mat with a thin, even coating (a slight thinning with water helps). After the adhesive has dried completely, the fabric can be attached by pressing with a warm iron to reactivate the glue. This method can also be used with dry-mount tissue. It is best to have a dry-mount press but you can also use a warm iron for this purpose. Seal dry-mount tissue is a good product for this.

If you have difficulty obtaining special glues, the ordinary white polyvinyl glues such as Elmer's will do. Of those commonly available in hardware stores, the best for our purposes is Sobo; it remains flexible and doesn't have a tendency to curl the board. Whichever glue is used, however, it is best to dry the mat under light pressure. A section of particle board or other dense panel (¾" [1.91 cm] or more) is useful as a press.

The velvets require a little extra consideration. You should never attempt to lift this type of fabric once it has been pressed into the glue, or tiny loops of nap will remain on the board and you'll have a bare spot on the support weave. In all covering procedures, you must be immaculate in your working habits. One spot of glue and everything must be done over! There is no way a spot can be cleaned; it just gets worse. Always apply the glue with the mat lying on waste paper and discard the paper at each turning. Newspaper will serve this purpose in many cases, although I wouldn't suggest it for white linen or other light-colored fabrics. The ink might transfer, so have plain wrapping paper or a clean sheet of newsprint available for this purpose.

After placing the velvet against the glue-coated surface, smooth the entire mat by gently rubbing in the direction of the nap. Examine the surface in the light to see that there are no places where the nap does not lie properly. Then allow the fabric to dry before turning the mat face down to fold the edges over on the back. Immediately after smoothing I usually pick the mat up, and touching only the underside, transfer it to a clean paper to dry. I do so because often in the smoothing process a little glue will have run under the edge of the bevel; and if allowed to dry, the glue would adhere the mat to the paper at the bevel's edge.

For small mats, apply the fabric to the glue-coated surface, laying the mat face down on the back of the fabric, then turn it back face up onto a fresh sheet of waste paper. This eliminates the glue that may have been brushed over the edges.

The gluing and application of fabric to larger mats requires a somewhat different approach. First, roll most of the fabric into a loose roll. Next, apply the glue to the side of the mat nearest you and for a short distance up the two adjoining sides, leaving about an inch of fabric to fold over the back. Unroll the fabric down onto the mat and proceed to apply the glue just ahead of the roll. Then smooth the fabric against the glue. Now paint ahead a few more inches on both sides and continue to unroll the fabric, always being careful not to press the fabric into the last of the glue. By this I mean that you should always stay ahead of the roll with the gluing. When you approach the other side, you should apply glue to the entire side and finish smoothing the fabric.

The mat is now ready to be turned over onto the clean waste paper. Use scissors to trim the fabric, leaving an even flap of about ¾" (1.91 cm) all around. Clip the corners off at 45° to create a mitered effect when the flaps are pulled around back. This step is slightly different when covering a mat that is not glued on the front. In that case, make the fabric about 1½″ (3.8 cm) larger than the board all around, so that you have enough to pull; then as you glue down the edges, cut the miters and trim off excess right on the mat, using a razor blade. Paint the glue on about ½″ (1.27 cm) of the edge of one side, then firmly press the fabric into it. Turn the mat and repeat the operation on the opposite side, making sure that a slight tension on the fabric pulls it smooth. If there are creases or wrinkles in the fabric, iron it beforehand. After gluing the two sides, cut with a razor blade to create miters and a uniform overlap, proceed to do the two other sides. This will also work as an alternate way or method for the front-glued covering.

When you make a covered mat, you must consider the type of board to be used. For a single linen cover, for instance, I usually choose double-thick matboard (eight-ply); but for a silk or velvet mat with a gold-beveled undermat, I prefer single-weight matboard for the top mat and double-thick for the undermat. In some cases I like to go even heavier on the undermat in order to have a deeper level. Upson board is good for this. When cutting a heavy board such as Upson, it's necessary to make a number of passes with the knife.

If your fabric-covered mat is an overmat, it should be glued to the undermat to prevent it from slipping out of alignment. This can be done with white glue. Apply the glue sparingly and only in spots, not all over. Make a complete line near the window to keep the mats from separating at this point.

There are a number of different materials available that come already glued to matboard. These include various colors of linen, burlap, and even grass-cloth. They are sometimes cut commercially with mat cutter machines so that the blade penetrates the board but does not cut the fabric. The board is peeled away, and the fabric (often backed by the face ply of paper) is pulled over the bevel and glued on the back. Otherwise, the bevel is normally cut through the fabric exposing a ragged edge of fabric and the interior of the board on the bevel. I do not suggest the use of these boards for the small shop or do-it-yourselfers.

Paper can also be used as covering for matboard. A particular color charcoal paper may be just what you want but is not thick enough to use as a mat. You can cover mats by the same principle used for cloth; or, if you wish to cut through for the bevel, you may simply laminate an entire sheet of paper to the face of the board using the method for wet-mounting (see section on mounting). The system used for light-weight fabrics in which the glue is allowed to dry and then the fabric adhered with a warm iron works well for paper because it does not allow the paper to become wet.

When working with cloth and paper mats, try to avoid the use of heavy color and excessive texture. For example, I have never seen *anything* I would mat with grass-cloth. Burlap, perhaps, but no matter what color burlap starts out as, within six months it will fade to half its original intensity. When natural roughness is desired, jute canvas is a better choice. This material is available in art supply stores as a support for painting.

Most fabrics suitable for matting are available in ordinary fabric stores. There are also special picture framers suppliers in the larger cities who stock linens with extra sizing and silks adhered to paper backing that make the covering process easier; but usually these fabrics are not available in small quantities—and they are not necessary. Just as the silks need not be real silk, linens need not be real linen. Butcher's linen works very well.

1 Cut the fabric larger than the mat and roll it into a loose roll. Apply the glue at the near edge and a short distance up the adjoining sides. Place the roll and smooth the fabric against the glue. Proceed to paint a distance up both sides of the mat and continue to unroll the linen.

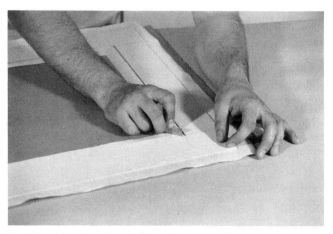

2 Turn the glued mat face down on clean scrap paper or board and cut out the center area with a razor blade. Carefully miter the corners with a razor blade. To prevent raggedness, avoid cutting too close to the corner.

3 Apply the paste to one side at a time, then pull the fabric over it.

THE COVERED MAT

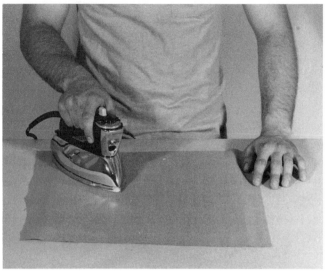

4 Be sure to pull firmly on the flaps around the window to insure a good edge on the bevel.

5 A warm iron and Poly-fab provide an alternate method of gluing. First apply Poly-fab adhesive to the mat. After the adhesive has dried completely, reactivate the glue by pressing the fabric with a warm iron.

Mixed media painting by Rex Clawson

A completed linen-covered mat.

THE OVAL MAT

Some pictures look best in oval or rounded mats. An old photograph, particularly a portrait that has been vignetted or dodged around the edges, looks especially good in an oval mat. Such a photograph has been chosen here to demonstrate the method of cutting and covering an oval mat. An undermat with a gilded bevel is also used.

There are special machines for cutting ovals and circles, but, because they are expensive, these machines are usually found only in professional shops and studios. However, a knife is sufficient to cut virtually any shape desired.

The first step in making an oval mat is to determine the size of the opening. For this photograph, an 8″ × 10″ (20.3 × 25.4 cm) opening seems to work well. Add the mat width to determine the overall size. I seldom add much more than 1½″ (3.8 cm) to an oval or circle; otherwise the corners look too large. For this mat I have chosen to add 1″ (2.54 cm) to the top and sides and 1¼″ (3.17 cm) to the bottom.

Cut two matboards—one for the top mat and one of double thickness for the undermat—to a size of 10″ × 12¼″ (25.4 × 31 cm). Using a marking block and rule, find the center of the top mat and draw a vertical line of axis. As you turn the mat, establish the point of intersection of the horizontal axis and draw a second line. Now mark the location of the top, bottom, and sides of the oval. Place the point of a compass at the intersection of the vertical (long) and horizontal (short) lines, and set the compass to the vertical radius. Now move the point of the compass to one of the outer points of the short line and swing the compass to cross the long line at two points to establish focal points. An oval can, of course, have any proportions, but I suggest avoiding extremely elongated shapes. The most pleasing shapes seem to be in the ratio of 8″ × 10″, 9″ × 12″, and 11″ × 14″ (20.3 × 25.4, 22.8 × 30.4, and 27.9 × 35.5 cm).

Having established the two focal points, place the mat on a scrap piece of board and put a push pin at each point. Also place a pin in the bottom opening point. Using button or carpet thread, or some similar nonstretching cord, tie a loop around the top focus and bottom opening pins. Include the bottom focus pin within the loop. Be sure to tie the string in a square knot to avoid slippage. Now pull out the bottom pin and place the point of the pencil in the loop. Apply slight tension with the pencil as you swing the thread along the line of the oval. Try to move in a smooth, counterclockwise direction from beginning to end. There are more complicated ways of plotting ellipses, but this method was advocated by Euclid.

Remove the pins and, keeping the mat on the scrap board, insert the matknife. Hold the knife at about 60° (30° off vertical). Cut exactly on the line as you move the knife and the mat. Since you are rotating the board, your hand will remain more or less in the same position, which makes it easier to maintain the bevel. (Some people use the Dexter cutter to make ovals. Although the Dexter cutter does make it easier to maintain the angle, it also makes following the line more difficult.) After cutting, sand away small imperfections with 220 sandpaper.

Now place the mat on top of the undermat and trace the oval. The oval of this undermat will have the same proportions as the mat. If I wanted the undermat lip to extend beyond the opening of the mat, I would draw a smaller oval on the undermat, following the procedure outlined above.

Gold leaf is going to be applied to the mat, so it should first be gessoed. Only true gesso is used by framers and gilders. True gesso consists of animal glue (usually rabbit skin glue) and whiting or chalk. Some mixes of true gesso contain white pigment as well, and some contain small amounts of plaster. These mixtures must be combined with water and heated in the top of a double-boiler. They do not keep unless refrigerated, and even when refrigerated, they do not last long. True gesso is the only really satisfactory ground for water gilding with real gold. (There is more information about water gilding in the framing section.) When oil gilding—which is what we'll be doing here—casein paint is an effective substitute for true gesso. Using casein makes it possible to eliminate the difficult and time-consuming process of making gesso. Casein paint (which is derived from milk solids) dries to a sandable, almost plasterlike hardness. The casein paint that is used here is not artists' casein paint, which is sold in tubes and is unsuitable for our purpose. I am using casein paint that is sold in cans (quarts and gallons) and is widely used in scenic painting for the theatre. These paints are sometimes referred to as "fresco" colors. They are water-based, dry quickly, and sand beautifully.

Sometimes I use only white, which simulates gesso. More often I use a red that resembles the red bole used for gilding. Two coats of this mixture should be applied to the bevel. The top coat should be allowed to dry thoroughly and should be lightly sanded. The second coat should just be rubbed with a soft cloth, to flatten the finish, and then sealed. Crystal Clear Krylon in spray can form is an excellent sealant. If you prefer to apply sealant with a brush, shellac works well. What is required is a totally nonabsorbent surface.

After the surface has been sealed, apply a coating of quick-size. Quick-size is a linseed oil varnish with japan drier. Sometimes the size is sold as "Japan Gold Size." The label should specify that the product "sets" in one to three hours, and that it has an "open" time of about three hours. In other words, the size should retain its tack long enough to

THE OVAL MAT

hold real gold. Quick-size must be tested after one hour to see if the tack has been reached. Test by touching the surface with the knuckle of your middle finger. If your knuckle comes away clean, and if there is a ticking sound, the size is ready. If the size is not ready, let it dry thirty minutes longer and test it again.

When the tack is right, lay the leaf. This is done by folding back the first page of a book of gold leaf enough to expose about ½″ (1.27 cm) of the first leaf of gold. Using this folded back edge of the book as a guide, cut the gold with a simple pass of the straight blade of a knife. You can use a gilding knife, such as the one shown here, but any sharp, straight blade will do.

After cutting the leaf, pick it up with a gilder's tip. The gilder's tip is first brushed through the hair in order to pick up a charge of static electricity, and also a little oil; thus the leaf adheres to the gilder's tip until it is transferred to the sized area. When the gold comes in contact with the sized area, it usually falls in place. Proceed in this manner until all the gold is transferred, and the entire bevel is laid.

The gold is now brushed down with a soft bristle brush. I use an oxhair lettering brush. Because the gold will not be handled or exposed to exterior exposure, it needs no protective coating.

Now the mat is ready to be covered. Oval and circular mats require special techniques. The cloth used here is moleskin. Moleskin is a short-napped fabric that is similar to velveteen. Pollyfab paste, which is applied with a brush, is used. After the center is cut out of the moleskin, it is necessary to cut the 1″ (2.54 cm) flap into many tiny tabs so that the folded fabric will conform to the curve of the opening. Don't cut too close to the bevel; cut to about ⅛″ (.32 cm) off the edge. Paste the tabs onto the back of the mat, position the top mat over the gold bevel mat, and glue the two mats together.

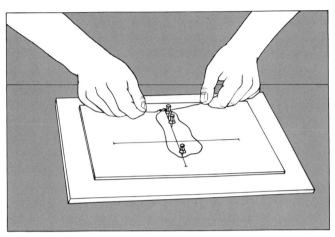

2 After placing pins at the two focal points and at the lower vertical radius point, tie a loop around the two outer pins. Use a square knot to avoid slipping.

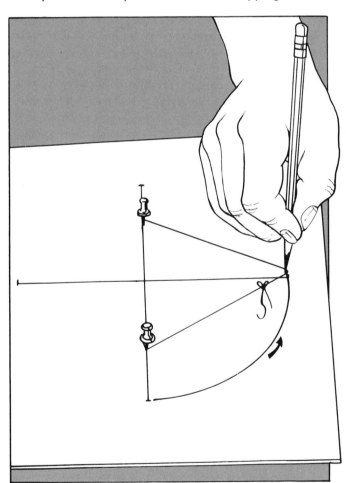

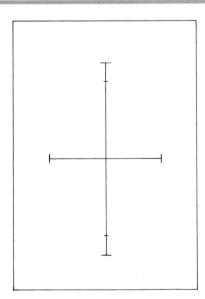

1 The focal points are established by placing the point of a compass at the intersection of the vertical and horizontal lines and setting the compass to the vertical radius. The compass point is then placed on the outer point of the horizontal line, and the two focal points marked.

3 Remove the pin from the lower vertical radius point, insert your pencil point in the loop, and swing the arc.

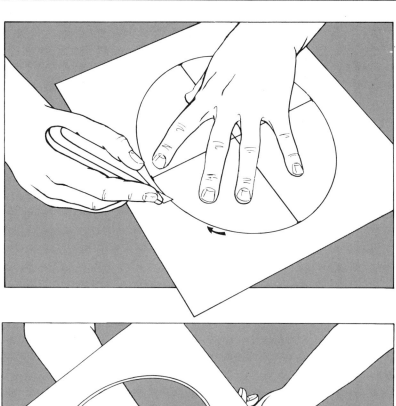

4 With the mat resting on a piece of scrap board, insert the knife at a 60° angle and cut. By simultaneously rotating the mat and pulling the knife, you can complete the cut while the knife remains more or less in the same position.

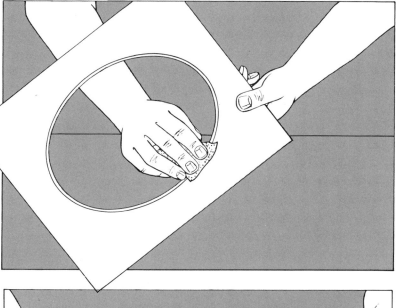

5 Use 220 sandpaper to smooth the cut and correct slight imperfections.

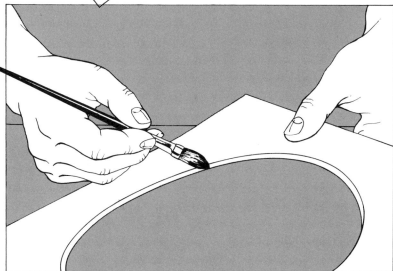

6 Apply goldsize to the bevel of the undermat, which has already been given two coats of red casein and two coats of white shellac.

7 Cut a piece of cardboard to the size of the book of gold leaf. Place the cardboard behind the book then cut the gold with a straight blade.

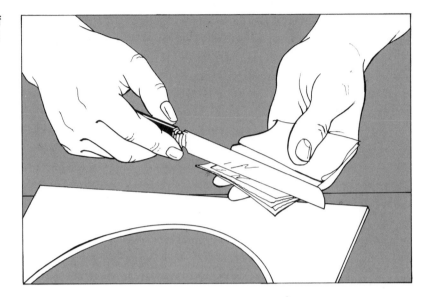

8 Brush the gilders tip through the hair to charge it with static. This will make the gold cling. Touch the flat side of the gilders tip to the cut strip of gold. Never try to pick up gold with your fingers.

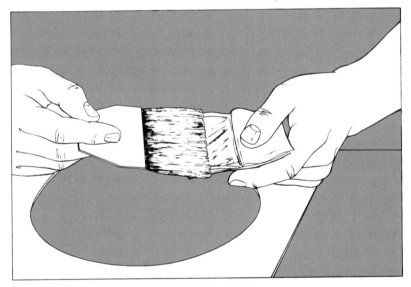

9 Transfer the gold to the sized bevel.

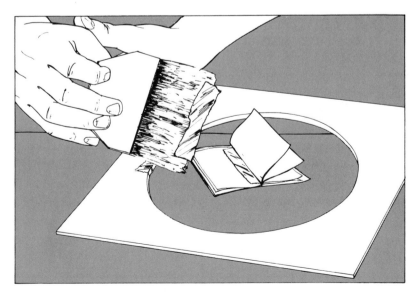

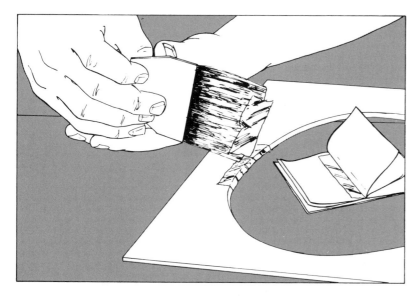

10 Lay the gold gently in place with the gilders tip. Try not to touch the size with the brush.

11 After all the gold is laid, pat it gently in place with a soft brush; here an oxhair lettering brush is used.

12 Place the glued mat face down on the back of the fabric.

13 After smoothing the fabric down, turn the mat over, trim the excess to an even order, and clip the corners to 45°.

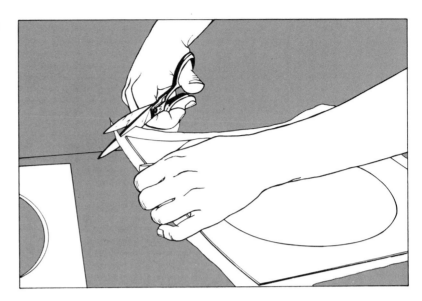

14 Apply paste to the edges of the fabric and neatly fold edges over the mat.

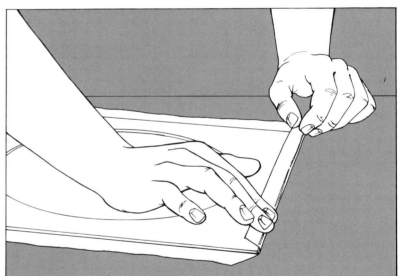

15 With the mat resting face down on a piece of scrap board, cut the center opening with a razor blade. Leave about 1″ (2.54 cm) margin of fabric.

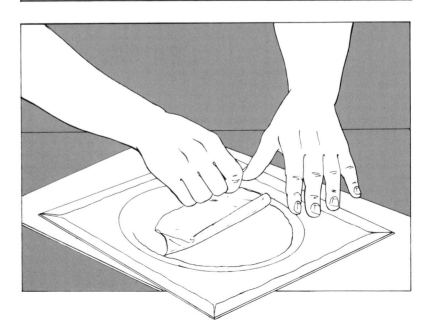

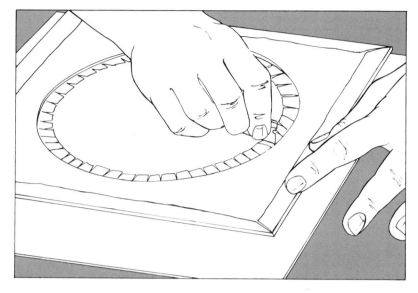

16 Cut the flap into many small tabs that will conform to the shape of the oval.

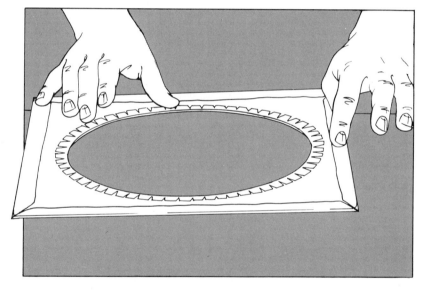

17 Paste the tabs down on the back of the mat.

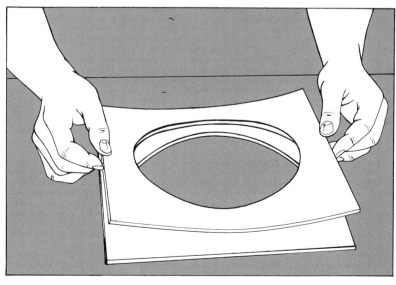

18 Position the top mat over the gold bevel mat and glue the two in place. Use glue sparingly.

THE FRENCH MAT

The French mat is probably the most decorative form of matting, the layered mat runs a close second, and inlay mats are third. (Inlay mats are outside the territory of this book because they require machines to produce.) A French mat is essentially a mat with lines on it forming additional frames or borders for the window. Some French mats are relatively simple and have only one or two lines of varying width set at intervals from the opening. Others are very elaborate incorporating many colors, including gold or silver.

The lines of the French mat are ordinarily drawn with a ruling pen and drawing ink. The washes can be watercolor or gouache, sometimes touched-up with pastel. They can also include applique in the form of thin gold foil lines or wider strips of materials such as hand-marbleized paper or even ribbons. Matting, like any other art, is often a matter of personal touch. I have seen Godey book prints framed very tastefully with strips of delicately colored satin ribbon. And combining marbleized endpapers and gold foil strips can make a very handsome mat.

The French mat becomes an integral part of the piece of art that you are matting. Therefore, this method works best on pieces I consider minor work, such as antique floral or fruit prints or decorative motifs from earlier days. The only times I have found French matting pleasing for more serious art is when very subtle color effects or combinations are used, such as two or three sanguine ink lines on a tan mat used to frame a sanguine ink or chalk drawing, or a gray ink line or two on a gray mat on a gray wash drawing. But, in general, the more contemporary in feeling the art is, the less inclined I would be to use a French mat.

The extremely decorative form of the French mat is an art in itself. I have seen lovely mats done for charming watercolors in which the picture and the mat added up to a fifty-fifty collaboration to create truly beautiful decorative objects. On the other hand, I would not surround a beautiful study by Watteau with a very fussy mat.

The method for cutting the French mat is the same one used for cutting a simple folder mat. In this case, however, I suggest cutting before "Frenching." First, select a suitable color for the base tone. You can use pale soft shades, although the idea of the standard French mat comes from decoration applied to the surface of cream-colored rag mats. Then cut out the opening. There are at least two ways to mark the lines. Some people measure from the edge of the mat making marks and then connecting them with penciled lines. Another way is to use a combination square, placing the sliding rule so that a 2″ (5.08 cm) mark strikes the very corner of the window when you have the 45° side of the square held against the edge of the mat. Make the measurements in fractions of inches as you move out from the window. Place just one dot at each point and be careful not to pierce the mat too much with the pencil. Keep a small scrap of paper or board by you as you measure and mark the first corner. Write on it the location of the dots so you will be able to repeat it on the other corners. On an even-bordered mat, you could put a strip of tape along the rule and mark it to help you recall the spots; but on a mat with a wider bottom, you will have to turn the square over anyway to keep from reading from the bottom edge.

If this procedure seems complicated, it isn't, and a little practice will show you how quickly you will be able to make acceptable French mats. Connect the dots with pencil lines, then rule in all the lines with the same color, say brown or gray. A watercolor wash can then be laid between the two lines. If you use watercolor the ink should be waterproof. If you plan your wash in gouache, the inking must be done after the wash because the pigmentation will fog the line. Gold ink lines can be added but narrow foil strips look better. In the example shown here, I have used ³⁄₃₂″ polyester tape. It is self-adhesive and is sold by picture framer supply houses. I have found that this type of mat looks best if most of the lines occur near the window and a sizable portion of mat remains toward the outside edge.

Bevels are not ordinarily colored; but there are really no rules in this regard. Corrections can be made in small mistakes or run-outs from the wash by scraping with a razor blade. This works best on ragboard. Chartpack makes tiny tapes in various colors, and the tape ordinarily used to stripe automobiles might also be used.

To lay in a wash, it is necessary to have fairly good brushes as well as a good bit of confidence. There are two ways of doing the wash. One is to simply apply it to the dry board, the other is to first apply a wash of clear water followed immediately by the watercolor. The second method affords a little more control over the starting and ending of the wash. The wash is most easily applied in a somewhat vertical position on an inclined board. A piece of thick matboard attached across the board will act as a stop for the edge of the mat and will still leave you freedom for turning the mat as you pass from one side to another.

Before you lay in the wash, mix the color and test it on a scrap piece of the same matboard. You cannot tell what color you have until after it has dried. When all is ready, carefully lay in a wash as quickly as you can. Charge the brush with water and make a small puddle that "hangs" on the board between the two lines. Then, using the tip of the brush, drag the puddle across and down, adding water as needed. Don't allow the puddle to dry up. As soon as you reach the end squeeze out the brush and pick up the puddle with it. Charge the brush with the color and repeat the operation, starting at the point where you left off; this will help the color to bleed.

Although some people prefer chisel-point lettering brushes for washes, I prefer to use a pointed watercolor sable brush that is at least a number 8 or larger. The watercolor paint may be either the pan or tube variety. The tubes are somewhat easier to use as they go into solution more easily, but be sure all the pigment is truly dissolved. It takes practice to lay a good wash. Do not be dismayed that there is variation in the tone; that is part of the beauty of a handmade wash—otherwise the stripes could be pasted on or airbrushed in. Textured mats and pulpboard are not very suited to the application of washes.

The biggest problem concerning the application of washes comes when you have to end the wash. I've found that it's best not to stop exactly at a corner of the mat. Go an inch or two around this corner when you begin; this will give you a straightaway when you are finishing. When the puddle starts to form, quickly rinse your brush and squeeze it out or stroke it on paper towels and use it to pick up the last of the color. Try not to overlay on the wash and never try to go back. If you think it isn't right, let it dry and retouch it with pastels and lightly spray with fixative.

1 Make a mat in the usual way. Mark for lines by placing dots along the corner edge at a 45° angle.

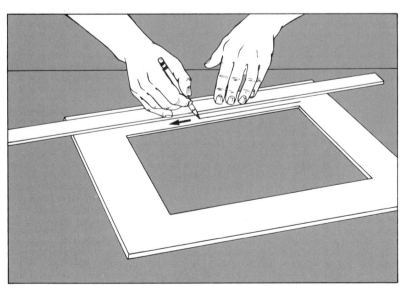

2 Connect the dots with pencil lines to form the basic structure of the French mat.

3 Lay the gold tape line along the first penciled line.

4 Ink in the lines with a ruling pen. If waterproof drawing inks are used, this step can be done either before or after the wash is laid. The transparent quality of watercolor allows the line to show through.

5 Lay in a plain water wash first. Follow with a watercolor wash. Tilt the drawing board sufficiently to let gravity assist you in the flowing of the wash.

6 If gouache is used for the wash, the inking of the lines must be done after the wash is completed. Otherwise, the gouache pigment will obscure the ink line.

This late eighteenth-century lithograph, *Tallien*, by Jean Lambert is ideally suited for a French mat.

THE GLASS MAT

This part of our section on matting and the one that follows on passe-partout are both concerned with the use of glass independent of framing. Glass mats start out like any other mat. First you measure for the opening and then you add the agreed upon width of mat to determine the outside dimensions of the mat, which in this case is glass.

Glass mats have not been fashionable for a long time, but they are very beautiful and perhaps due for a revival. Although the possible variety of the glass mat is endless, the example shown here is the classic type, which is the type often found on English hunting prints where the hunters in their red jackets are nicely complemented by the gold and black glass.

After you determine the size of the opening and add the appropriate width to all sides, it's time to cut the glass. (Look at the glass cutting part of the framing section on pages 86–87.) Not that you will necessarily cut your own glass, but you should at least become familiar with the process. It is quite easy to master if you feel so inclined, or you may simply have your local glazier cut it to size.

Next thoroughly clean the glass. Use a good cleanser like Bonami, followed by alcohol and a dry cloth. In any case, the glass should be "squeaky-clean," so try to avoid touching the surface with your fingers. Using the marking block, abut the edge of the glass and the end of the ruler to it. Then apply tape to the back side of the glass at the approximate place for the opening. Overlap the tape in both directions, because it is impossible to apply tape in straight lines on the glass surface. To mark the points showing the dimensions of the opening on the tape use the marking block and folding rule. The straight-edge and knife can be used to cut the excess tape. Then peel it away and leave only the opening "masked." Repeat the operation as many times as needed to create the next line of masking on the glass. I should point out here that the masking can work either way. The method I use here masks out the gold lines. You can, of course, mask in the black background and do the gold lines first. There are differing opinions on this, even among people who have practiced this art for a long time.

But, no matter which method you use, the gold will always have to be laid twice and there will always be touch-up with the black; but this is a beautiful mat when properly done. The type of tape used can be important. Clear scotch tape works well, drafting tape is also good, but ordinary masking tape doesn't work as well.

After you have done the necessary masking for the glass mat, the next step is dependent on which area—the stripe or the background—you have masked. If you are using the method shown here, you need to paint the exposed glass areas with black japan-color or black enamel mixed with a little varnish (asphaltum varnish is the classic choice for this, but other varnishes will do as well). Allow this black coating to dry, then peel the tape away. If the line is not perfect, correct it with a brush and razor blade. Use the brush to paint in black where needed and the razor blade to scratch out black that has found its way under the masking.

When the black coating is dry (the next day is best), apply the gold. This method of application of gold is the same one used for gold lettering on store windows. Since the gold is being laid from the back, it cannot have a perceptible adhesive or "size" to adhere it to the glass, thus it cannot be laid with ordinary gold size as in our other examples of gilding. Glass gilding requires a special size that allows the gold to lie flat against the glass and create a mirrorlike surface. Two substances can be used for this—fish glue and gelatin capsules.

The example shown here is done with gelatin capsules, which means that two gelatin capsules (just the empty capsules, that is) should be dissolved in one cup of boiling water. When they are dissolved, add another cup of cold water, which will make a full pint. There are those who argue that it should be used hot. There are other variations suggested, too, such as if a teaspoonful of grain alcohol is added, the life of the size will be prolonged. But since grain alcohol is difficult to obtain, you can simply make new size when you need it (it keeps somewhat longer in the refrigerator). Gelatin capsules can also be difficult to obtain. You may be able to get them from your local pharmacy or from health-food stores that sell them to improve the quality of their customers' nails.

The alternate size most commonly used is fish glue. It normally comes in flake form and requires a piece the size of a quarter to be dissolved in a pint of water. As in the gelatin capsule method, it is best to dissolve the glue in one cup of boiling water and add a cup of cold water to make the pint. After thorough stirring of this solution, strain the size through a coffee filter into a clean jar with a lid. The fish glue goes bad so rapidly that it needs to be made fresh on the day it is used.

Apply the size with a soft, well-charged brush, letting it flow freely from left to right, completely covering the lines on one side of the mat. Then quickly, while the size remains wet, cut and lay the gold. Double XX gold for surface gilding is the type of gold used for this operation. Because it is too delicate to be handled with the fingers, it must be picked up and laid using a gilder's tip. This is a wide flat brush made with a cardboard handle. (This process has already been shown in the oval mat section on pages 37–43).

But for whatever small variations there are here, a brief discussion is required. First, hold the book of gold in one hand with the first pages folded back to reveal the sheet of gold. To make the cutting easier, it's best to support the book with a piece of cardboard or matboard cut to the size of the book. Then, with a straight-bladed knife, move gently across the sheet of gold. Next, brush the gilder's tip through your hair to pick up oil and static. When the tip is laid against the gold, the cut strip should adhere to the side of the brush. Place it on the beginning of the line you have sized and gently lower it into place. Try not to touch the size with the brush. Cut and lay another piece with a little overlapping. Continue as rapidly as possible to complete the laying of all the gold on this side of the mat before the size dries. Do not attempt to patch or pat the leaf into place as it will make a terrible mess. Turn to the opposite side of the mat and repeat the operation, gilding the adjacent sides one at a time.

Let everything dry thoroughly, preferably overnight. Using a ball of sterile cotton, polish the back of the gold to make it flatter and brighter. Look at it from the front to really see the brightness level and check for flaws. Then, having wiped away any excess gold, apply the size again in the same manner and while it is wet, lay gold on the missing spots. Let this second gilding dry overnight and the next day

burnish the gold again with a ball of cotton.

Next comes the washing. Dip the brush in the size and flood the back of the gold another time. This will brighten the gilt and, if desired, can be done more than once. After it has dried, the gold is ready for backing. Chrome yellow japan-color works well for this when mixed with a little turpentine and some varnish to act as a binder. When this mixture is dry you may want to finish the job with a coating of japan black mixed the same way. This step is not necessary; it is done only to eliminate the messy effect of yellow strips on the back.

Of course, black and gold need not be the only choice of decoration on the back of the glass. Japan-colors are also not the only choice. Acrylic lacquer in spray cans is a possible substitute; gold does not have to be used at all. Black and white can give pleasing results. Household enamels can be used, though their drying time is quite long. Silk-screened designs could be considered if you are thinking of producing a number of identical mats.

1 Apply gelatin size to the clear glass lines that remain on the black painted mat.

2 Using the gilders tip, lay a gold strip on the wet size.

3 Continue to lay in the gold strips, overlapping each one on the one before.

THE
NO-MAT
MAT

The no-mat look is created with two panels of glass, which lets the trim that extends beyond the art serve as the "mat." Thus the color of the wall becomes the color of the mat. The no mat can be done with wooden frames, but I am taking this opportunity to show you the use of a metal section frame. These metal frames might be said to have become the frame of our era. I don't care much for them, but they have their place and should be shown in this book. Some people claim that these "do-it-yourself" frames are easy to assemble. I rather think they are not. However, with patience and enough time you will be able to assemble one of these modern wonders in a satisfactory manner. There are a number of brands on the market and they are available in most art supply stores. The "kit" consists of two packages (boxes or plastic sleeves), each containing two strips of frame section of a given length. So if you wish to make a frame to fit a mat measuring 14" × 18" you should purchase one package of each dimension. The necessary hardware for assembly and hanging is included in each package. Some types come with an Allen wrench, but other types may require the use of an ordinary slotted screwdriver or perhaps a number 1 or 2 Phillips head screwdriver. Usually these frames are available only in even inches, but I have found stores that will cut them to odd sizes. Most of the time you will be able to absorb the difference in the mat, but if you are framing "close," that is, without a mat it could be a problem.

In the example shown here, I have chosen an oil on paper to sandwich between glass. I chose the no-mat look because it seemed to me that this piece calls for a light, airy look. The piece measures 14" × 17" (35.5 × 43.18 cm). I have chosen a 20" × 24" (50.8 × 60.9 cm) frame for it, which seems to leave sufficient breathing room around the

piece and still keeps the frame to a manageable size. I would not recommend this method for pieces that are much larger.

Section frames are available in a variety of finishes. They hark back to a prototype aluminum frame with welded corners and polished face that was first made popular by the artist-framer Robert Kulicke, who did frames for the Museum of Modern Art. By the mid-sixties these frames, which were very elegant, were all the rage. Then came the do-it-yourself section frame, which although inferior, still creates a cool, clean look very suited to our times. In the example shown, I have chosen the gold anodized finish (all of these frames are aluminum) because I feel this particular piece looks better in gold than in silver. (In the following section I use a black section frame.)

Because the painting is sandwiched between two sheets of picture glass, the space in the aluminum extrusion that serves as a rabbet will not be filled. This problem would ordinarily be taken care of by the insertion of spring clips in the back, but here they would be unsightly. Nor is it possible to pad it out by the use of additional backing to fill the space, because in this case there is no backing. So I have used strips of wood painted black. The strips measure 3/16" × 1/4" (.48 × .64 cm). They are slid into the frame from the front, on the face of the glass. This creates a neat black line all around that looks very handsome.

In the process of assembling the frame put three sides together, then slide the double glass that has been taped together with scotch tape into the rabbet and apply the fourth side. Be sure to follow the directions for the assembly of the particular frame you have, since directions vary and corner connections are often tricky.

When hanging your piece, I suggest you hang it by the frame itself and not use the supplied hangers. To hang it yourself, look for the groove in the back of the extrusion (at least in this brand) into which you can insert the head of a four-penny nail. This means that great care must be taken when driving the nails into the wall for hanging. The nails should be rather far apart but not in the very corners of the frame so as to allow room for side-to-side adjustment. They also must be absolutely level, since there is no leeway factor as there is in the case of hanging with a wire over two nails. A small spirit level of the sort used by masons can be very useful. It can rest on a piece of wood that has been placed on the first nail driven. Move the stick up and down, letting it pivot on the nail until the bubble in the level is centered, then drive the other nail just at the bottom edge of the stick. Do not measure down from the ceiling or up from the floor to find the two nail positions as floors and ceilings are notorious for being out of level, even in the newest buildings.

For this type of hanging I use "common" nails; "box" nails also work well. Nails come in many varieties but there are two major divisions: common, or nails with heads; and finishing, which means nails that have small ball-like heads. Finishing nails are thinner and are the ones used for most picture hanging, but for this purpose it is nice to have the head of the nail catch inside the edge of the space in the back of the metal extrusion. Because of the limited space in the back of the frame the nails must be driven farther into the wall than they would be for ordinary hanging.

To make the "sandwich" for insertion into this type of frame, you should have two sheets of picture glass of equal size. Avoid using single-strength window glass; the piece will be heavy enough even with the thinner picture glass. Window glass is also not as optically clear as picture glass and will tend to "green" the mat area. Wash both pieces of glass on both sides. Handle them gingerly by their edges so as not to spot them with fingerprints. Water should be all you need to wash the glass. Use a damp cloth and a dry one to polish. Rub vigorously with the damp one, then rub the glass dry until you hear a squeeky sound. This should be done with the glass lying flat on the table on a paper-covered surface. Then place the art on one sheet and measure for an even border. When you feel satisfied with the placement raise one of the upper corners and place a "roll" of tape behind it to hold the paper in place against the glass. Note that the "roll" or loop of tape is made around the end of the finger with the "sticky side" out. It should be applied with consideration given to the direction to prevent it from unrolling. In the example shown, the tape is specially made for picture framing and has a neutral pH. Other types of tape might be used so long as they adhere to both the work and the glass. Spray mounts are another possibility.

Now put the second glass carefully in place and, pulling one edge of the sandwich over the edge of the table, proceed to apply ½" (1.27 cm) clear tape to the edges, overlapping about ³⁄₁₆" (.48 cm) front and back. You might use the straight-edge as a guide, but in this case it was not necessary because the tape is transparent. The balsa wood strips used to wedge the glass in place are available from model makers suppliers and may be painted with black japan-color oi with India ink. Of course, they could also be done in any color.

If the strips are mitered to fit the rabbet, they must be inserted when the frame is assembled. If they are cut square to fit the opening, the strips can be inserted after the frame is assembled. There are advantages to both ways. The mitering causes you difficulty in the assembly, but it holds the molding in place. The butt joining after the frame is together is easier but may leave you having to glue two sides into the rabbet.

1 After thoroughly cleaning the glass by rubbing it with a cloth dampened with water, and following that by brisk rubbing with a dry cloth, carefully position the artwork. Leave even borders on the sides but give a wider space at the bottom than the top, to allow for visual drop.

2 When you have determined the correct position, lift one corner of the paper, taking care not to move the art. Then place a small ring of self-adhesive tape onto the glass, so that the top corner of the picture covers the tape.

3 After the top piece of glass is in place, apply clear plastic tape to the edge of the sandwich. This will keep the two pieces of glass from moving and also serve as a dust seal.

4 Screw the two side sections together with the top piece of the section frame. (Different brands of section frames have slightly different joining systems for the corners.) When all sides have been joined, slide the sandwich into the rabbet, and place the bottom section in position and tighten the screws.

5 Finally, inspect the work and remove fingerprints from the glass before hanging.

PASSE-PARTOUT

Passe-partout might be said to belong to the framing part of the book. It is placed in the part on matting because passe-partout is not quite "framing." This method, in which a picture, a mat, a piece of glass, and some sort of backing are held together by strips of paper or cloth pasted over the edges, is used in Europe even for pieces that are being framed, primarily because it is a superior method of protecting a piece of art. In this country, passe-partout is more often a system used to substitute for a frame. And since there are so many alternate methods for exhibiting without frames available today, the art of passe-partout has almost disappeared.

Passe-partout takes more time to do than Swiss Clips or Clippity Strips or Braquettes, which are only a few of the many "fast frame" items on the market, but it has a long tradition and the finished piece may be kept and exhibited for many years. This is definitely not the case with the aforementioned products; they allow dust to enter between glass and mat. They are also very vulnerable because the edges of the glass are exposed.

To prepare for this method, first measure for the folder mat as you would in any other matting job. Add the appropriate mat widths and cut the window. You might also use the drop-on technique if allowing the picture to touch the glass is no problem. I have taken apart passe-partout photographs that were sealed for more than thirty years. The photographs had been mounted in the drop-on manner and put directly against the glass. Each glass bore the complete image of the photograph, yet the pictures did not appear to be damaged. I have also encountered this phenomenon in ordinarily framed pictures such as etchings and lithographs, and occasionally in a watercolor or gouache. I will not attempt to give you the scientific rundown on what causes this sort of "transfer," but I have noticed that the work itself had not suffered because of it. Works of art that really

should not touch the glass are those done in oil on paper or mixed-media pieces composed of various layers of lacquer, shellac, or acrylic medium. These substances can adhere themselves to the glass, and when separation is attempted damage often occurs.

A piece of glass and a piece of backing should be cut to fit the size of the mat. The usual material for the backing is ⅛" (.32 cm) chipboard. This is the gray pulpboard used to back drawing pads and such, it is not to be confused with "particle-board," which is a building supply item made of chips. The chipboard piece should lie behind the back of the folder mat, because it is not of a neutral pH. If you care to pay the price, there is a "rag" form of this board that is supposed to be neither acid nor alkaline. I have found no problem with the ordinary type so long as it is interfaced with a good quality mat or a sheet of rag paper.

The next step is to attach the passe-partout rings. These have become increasingly difficult to obtain, but they are still manufactured and sold through picture framing supply sources. However, many of these picture framing outlets do not do business with individuals; they only deal in large quantities. If you cannot obtain the rings at your local art supply store, you might improvise with any available small ring or a loop of wire and a bent strip of thin brass or aluminum. These will resemble the brass paper fasteners, with a ring instead of a head. There are also glue-on linen tabs with grommets; but I don't trust them because the adhesive on the tabs is not reliable. The brass strips of the classic ring actually penetrate the back and are folded on the other side.

For average-size art, mark the position for the rings about 1½" (3.8 cm) in from the sides and about 2½" (6.35 cm) down from the top. A wire will be placed between the rings, so the rings must be far enough down from the top to allow for a little slack. Make two small holes at these points using the tip of an X-Acto knife or similar small blade. Insert the brass prongs of the ring and fold them down in opposite directions on the inside. I like to give them a little tap with a hammer to flatten them and then cover them with a small piece of brown paper tape to keep the tips flat against the board. Next, place your matted art on top, and after washing the glass, position it correctly. Use ordinary water to clean the glass, and place the glass on a clean paper-covered surface, rubbing it well with a damp cloth. To polish, use a dry cloth. Then turn the glass, holding it by its edges, and clean the other side. If the glass is dirty, it might be necessary to add a little household ammonia to the water, but usually glass fresh from the glazier is quite clean.

By standing the sandwich on the table and lightly bouncing it, you can position all the elements to a proper alignment. At this point place temporary binding tabs of masking tape on three sides to hold everything in place. Now lay the untaped edge over the edge of the table and place the straight-edge on its surface about ⅛" (.32 cm) from the edge. The straight-edge can be held in place by spring clips or small clamps. Cut a strip of gummed linen tape (the traditional favorite) or some other tape of your choice. Apply it to the glass and pull it sharply down with your fingers to create a good clean edge, folding it over onto the back. With a razor, cut the ends even with the sandwich.

Now turn to the opposite edge and repeat. Be sure to apply the tape in the same order if you are doing more than one passe-partout, so that all lapping at the corners goes in the same direction. The addition of picture wire to the rings completes the job.

PASSE-PARTOUT

1 Insert the wings of passe-partout ring through ⅛″ (.32 cm) chipboard backing, flattening their ends with a hammer. Place small squares of gummed paper tape over them to keep the ends flat.

2 Turn the board over and attach picture wire to the rings. Keep the wire relatively taut across the back of the picture; too much slack will cause it to hang loose off the wall.

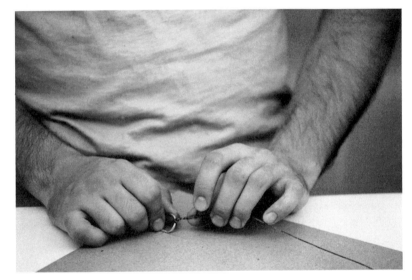

3 Place the edge of the sandwich— glass, folder mat, and backing—over the edge of the table. Then, using a straight-edge to guide the overlap, apply the linen tape.

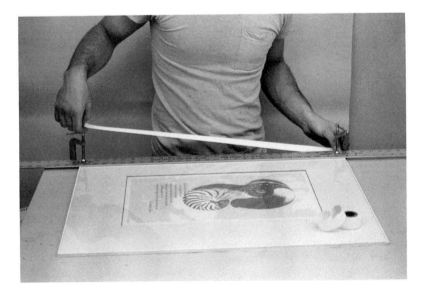

The completed passe-partout mat.

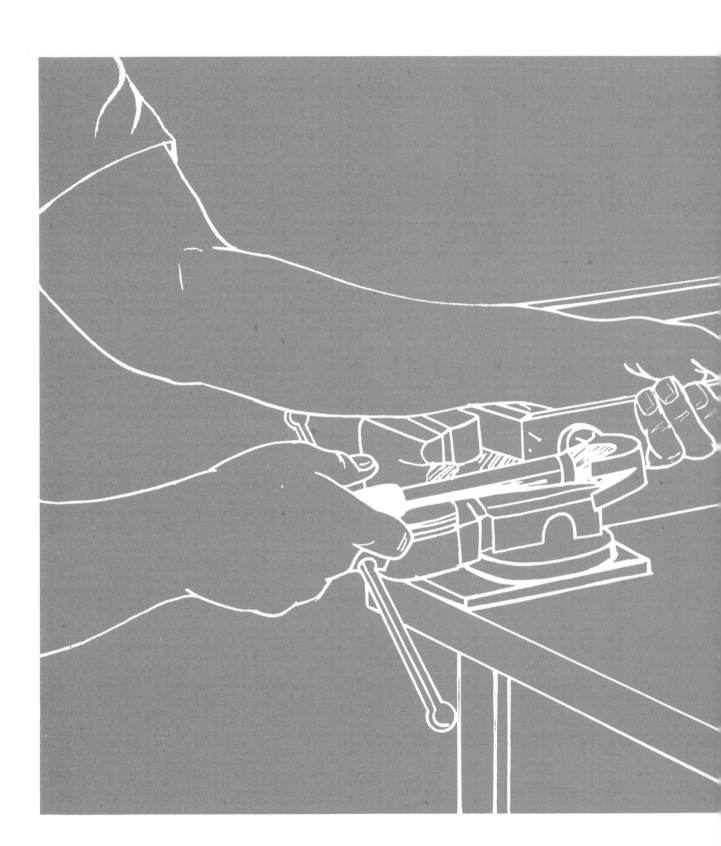

PART TWO

FRAMING

The framing of a work of art is the final and finishing touch that should set it apart from other pieces and objects in the world around it. Ideally, the framing should draw attention to the piece and enhance it; but in no way should it compete for your attention. Matting, of course, is part of the framing process and is of considerable importance, especially in the framing of the works considered in this book, which concentrates on works under glass. In this section, however, I will talk about the actual picture frames—that final piece of wood or metal molding that holds all the assembled parts of the framing sandwich in place. The frame should enhance, not dominate, the presentation; for this reason most frames should be of modest proportions and subtle finish. Very complex and ornamental frames are best reserved for paintings on canvas or panels, where the strength of the piece can compete with the frame and a harmonious whole can exist. A frame, like a setting for a fine jewel, should strike a proper balance between function and display. Frames need not be simple to do this, although often simplicity is the surest course.

The frame must first of all be physically capable of holding the piece. Too small a molding won't work on a large piece. Time and experience will teach the proper and most pleasing proportions. I suggest that the critical dimension, that is, the size at which the molding size becomes a serious matter for consideration, is 24″ × 30″ (60.9 × 76.2 cm). Almost any molding will work with anything smaller, and anything larger will require larger moldings and retainers.

Width and style of moldings are a matter of taste. I seldom like moldings wider than 1″ (2.54 cm); however, retainers, or strainers, as some people call them, allow the use of delicate frames on larger works. Ordinarily, I do not approve of this since I feel the frame should simply make its own statement about what is necessary. The frame should be saying, "I am this heavy because I'm necessary." As far as finish goes, the color, texture, or quality should echo something in the picture. Gold says rich and

opulent; ivory says warm and sensual; and black says crisp and clean. The driftwood effect suggests seascapes or landscapes, and a waxed finished natural wood works to harmonize with the tones in the piece.

Although an in-depth study of the art of framing is not within the province of this book, I would like to use this section for a brief discussion of the elementary types of frames used for framing artwork that has already been matted or protected by glass. Here, you will find tips that make it possible for you to make your own frames, using materials that are readily available. Pieces that are customarily matted require only rather small and simple frames. In these cases, the matting often constitutes a large portion of the "frame," and so I have included only a few very basic shapes in the diagram showing molding profiles. Most of these shapes are easily made if you have access to a table saw. Others must be milled commercially and are available in some lumberyards or picture framing supply stores. The larger and more elaborate moldings used for canvasses and paintings on panels have been left out.

The most universal molding shape is the "box." Box-style frames are simply a flat strip of molding turned on edge and then rabbeted to receive the picture. The "rabbet" is the L-shaped groove cut into one of the sides of a strip of molding; it forms a lip to catch the glass, mat, and backing. My favorite shape for medium-sized works of art is a box presenting a ½″ to ⅝″ (1.27 to 1.59 cm) face with a 1″ to 1¼″ (2.54 to 3.18 cm) back. Larger pieces might take ¾″ (1.91 cm) on the face and 2″ (5.08 cm) on the back. This is because a larger frame requires what is called a "strainer," or retainer, which is a secondary flat frame inserted into the frame behind the artwork. This flat frame is usually made of raw basswood with lap-jointed corners and fits into the back of the frame in order to carry the weight of the glass. It is usually 1¼″ to 2″ (3.18 to 5.08 cm) wide and whatever thickness will fit within the back of the frame, ½″ to ⅝″ (1.27 to 1.59 cm) perhaps.

The strainer is often attached to the outer

frame with screws, usually from the inside; but in this day of "high tech" the practice of having the screws show is popular, so the screws are put in from the outside. I prefer them on the inside. As to what particular size at which the strainer becomes necessary, I would say at about 24″ × 30″ (60.9 × 16.2 cm) there comes a point when you should strongly consider its use; certainly by the time you have reached the 30″ × 40″ (76.2 × 101.6 cm) category you are in the "must have" size. If the size goes beyond 40 inches—say to 48 inches—then a crossbar support is also a good idea.

The rabbeting remains the same no matter what size the molding is. The cut is usually about ³⁄₁₆″ (.48 cm); seldom do rabbets cut deeper than ¼″ (.64 cm). The distance from the face to the rabbet is also rather standard at about the same as the width of the rabbet. There are moldings that have rabbets set farther back but these are exceptions.

The molding diagram on page 60 shows the various shapes that can be combined from the standard moldings available at the lumberyard. Selecting a frame for a particular piece of art depends of course on your own taste. But there are some standards. The classical molding forms, such as the "colonial," are typically more suitable for pieces of a traditional nature. And with varying finishes this classic shape can be suited to many different kinds of pictures. The rounded tops of some of the flat and box styles and the flowing lines of the swan molding tend to give soft effects. The O'Keeffe is a molding shape made popular by the artist Georgia O'Keeffe, who used it to frame many of her paintings. She used glass for most of her oil paintings. A fair substitute for this style molding can be made by gluing small quarter round molding to create a rabbet. Look at the molding shapes in your local lumberyard and try to imagine their use as picture frames. After all, along with time and experience, it is your ability to envision new and aesthetically pleasing combinations that in time will determine your own personal style.

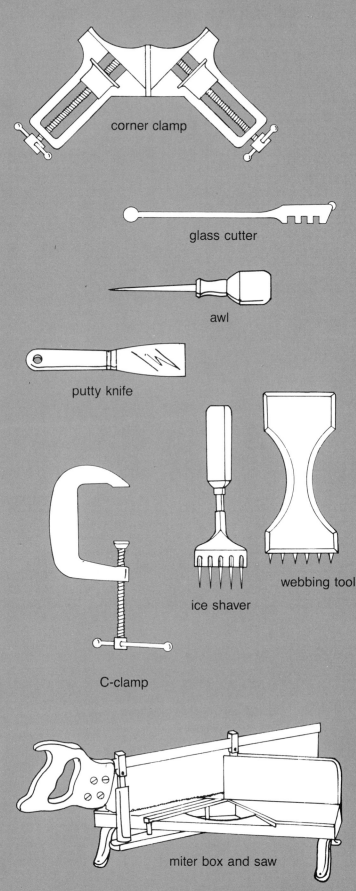

corner clamp

glass cutter

awl

putty knife

C-clamp

ice shaver

webbing tool

miter box and saw

MOLDING PROFILES

Moldings are merely lengths of wood shaped in some specific manner. In the chart shown here you can see the profiles of those molding types and styles most available to the home craftsman. The styles composed of rabbeted strips (that is, a relatively thin piece compared to its width) are known as "flats." Flats are arranged in both horizontal and vertical positions; each has quite a different effect. Occasionally you will see flats that have an added notch to create a lip.

In order to add variety to these standard shapes, you can tilt the table saw and create beveled sides or tops and thus make a whole new family of moldings. The more elaborate shapes require more sophisticated tools such as routers and are not always within most people's reach. However, many of these shapes, particularly the molded type of moldings, are available in lumberyards and framing supply shops. Sometimes these moldings have a rabbet, which makes them a suitable choice for picture framing; in other cases they need to have a rabbet cut into them, thus requiring the use of a table saw.

When two or more of the simple moldings are combined to form a more ornate frame, they are called compound moldings. The extent of these combinations is endless. By checking your local lumberyard, you will find many ordinary household moldings that lend themselves to framing.

When selecting a suitable molding for a particular piece of artwork, keep in mind that smaller works generally look best in wider moldings or in narrow moldings with wide matting. The point is that when a work is very small it requires emphasis, by the use of either a wide mat or a wide frame to draw attention to its special qualities. Otherwise, the small work can become lost and insignificant. By contrast, a large work will, by virtue of its sheer size, insist itself on our senses, thus requiring more minimal framing.

Flats are suitable for most works of art, especially when used with mats. When a vertical flat receives a rounded face, it becomes a round. Rounds are also very versatile. As moldings become wider and more ornamental, their use must be more carefully controlled so as not to overpower the artwork. When there is any question at all, it is always better to err on the side of brevity than to overstate. Understatement in framing is to be praised. How many times have we seen a botched framing job destroy delicate and otherwise noteworthy work. So when choosing a molding, keep it simple. If you feel inclined to use more ornament, go to a graceful swan or an O'Keeffe or a colonial, but steer clear of the very fussy and excessively ornamental styles. There will come the time, however, when you will feel the need to make a more flamboyant expression. By all means, do it! When I warn against overstatement, I am only making a generalization. I am not encouraging the relative safety of always choosing the safe and tried solution. Good framing solutions require analysis and thought.

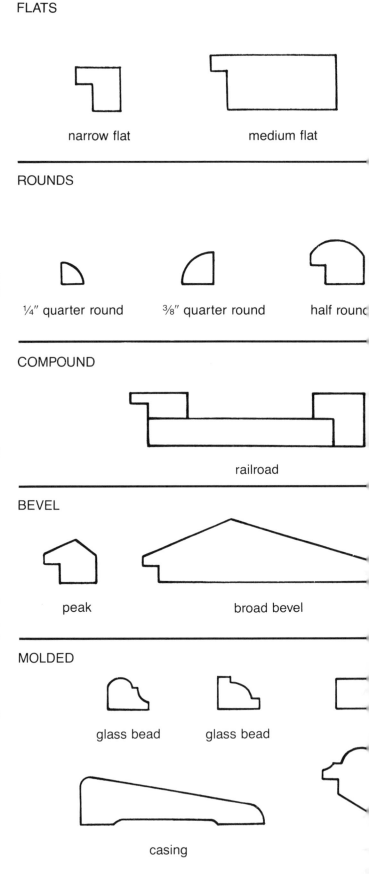

FLATS

narrow flat   medium flat

ROUNDS

¼" quarter round   ⅜" quarter round   half round

COMPOUND

railroad

BEVEL

peak   broad bevel

MOLDED

glass bead   glass bead

casing

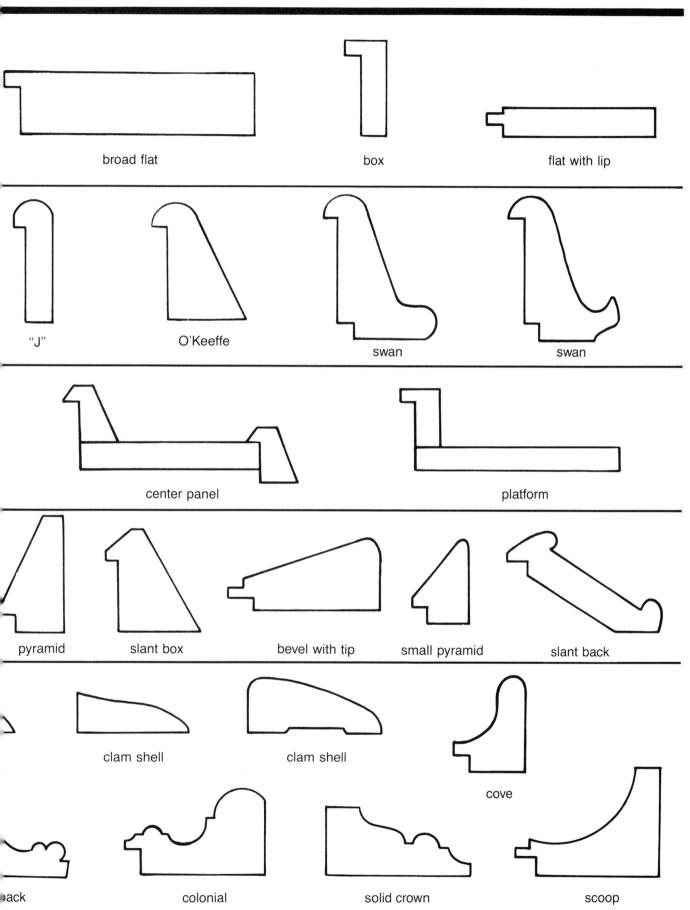

broad flat

box

flat with lip

"J"

O'Keeffe

swan

swan

center panel

platform

pyramid

slant box

bevel with tip

small pyramid

slant back

clam shell

clam shell

cove

back

colonial

solid crown

scoop

PUTTING IT ALL TOGETHER

On this and the following pages is shown a variety of matting and framing combinations. All of them are taken from the framed and matted pieces illustrated throughout the book. Included with each finished piece are a profile of the molding shape used and a cross section of the complete matting/framing/backing sandwich.

The purpose of this section is to show you the practical and aesthetic considerations that go into selecting a particular frame and mat for a particular piece of art. As you look over the various possibilities, note the variety of materials, molding silhouettes, textures, and how each frame carries out in some way the feeling expressed in the work it surrounds.

box

CROSS SECTION

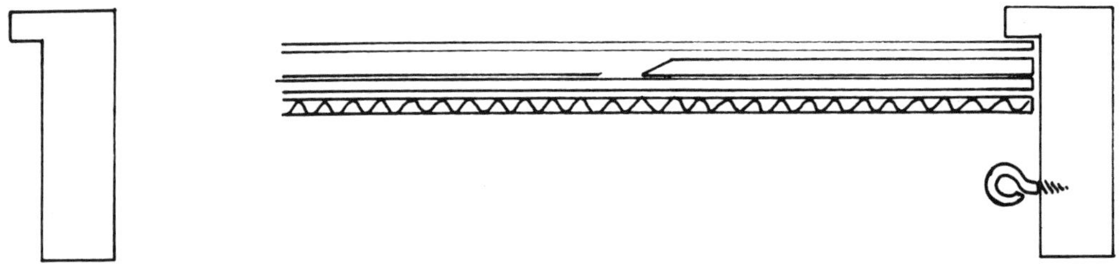

peak

"J"

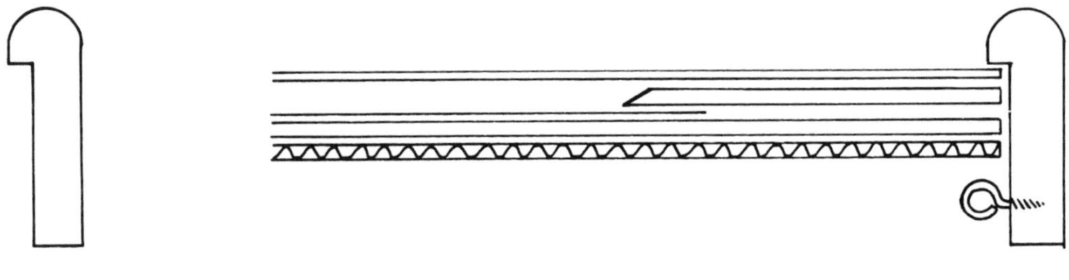

This gold metal-leafed, box-style frame was decorated on its face by the artist. So as not to cover any of the image, the painting was made to float on a museum-board backing inside the window of the mat. The entire arrangement is backed by corrugated cardboard for added rigidity. The mat is covered in white linen, which is often effective when used in combination with silver or gold frames of very simple shape. Strongly colored or heavy pictures such as this benefit from the use of linen mats but for more delicate pieces, the rough texture of linen could overwhelm the art. In general, it is a mistake to use linen mats on photographs, as they often require a simpler, more subtle setting.

Mixed media painting, Rex Clawson.

Here, a walnut peak-shaped molding effectively frames this small painting. Mounted on black matboard and backed with chipboard, the painting is placed directly against the glass because the depth of the molding doesn't allow for the use of a spacer strip. The painting, however, doesn't appear to have suffered any bad effects. Although many conservators warn against this practice of placing art next to glass, I have used this method without encountering any problems for thirty years. (Of course, pieces with sticky surfaces can't be done this way.) The black matboard works very well here to show off the vivid coloring of the painting, and it makes a handsome combination with the natural wax-finished walnut frame. Painting, Faye Coursey.

Its rounded face echoing the forms of the drawing, this life drawing looks very handsome in this gold, metal-leafed "J" molding. A tan mat (Bainbridge 412) with two brown ink lines near the opening complements the tones of the sanguine chalk and the color of the paper. Papers of lesser quality often turn brown with age and can be made to seem less so by using a darker mat. Because this drawing was done on newsprint and needed to be preserved, it was wet mounted on double-thick white matboard before it was matted. A sheet of corrugated cardboard gives needed added support. The frame, as with most of my metal-leaf finishes, was toned with a brown glaze to further harmonize with the art. Drawing, Romolo Costa.

PUTTING IT ALL TOGETHER

half round

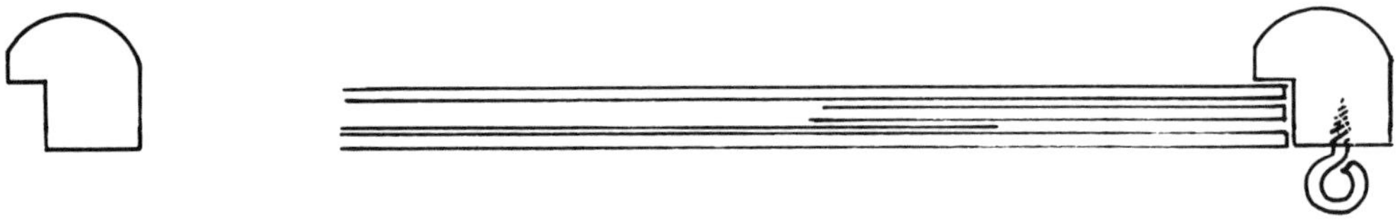

box

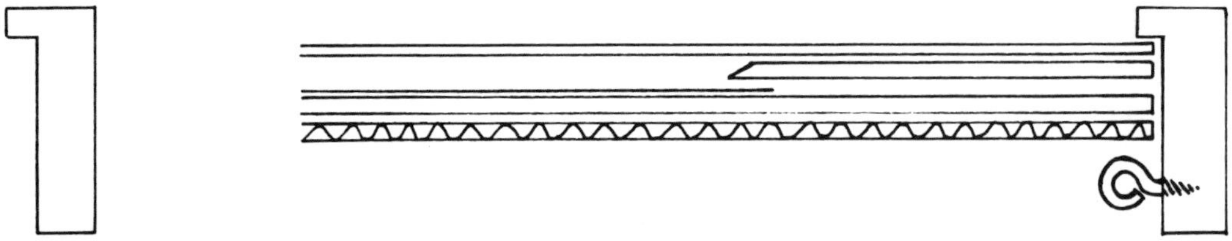

colonial

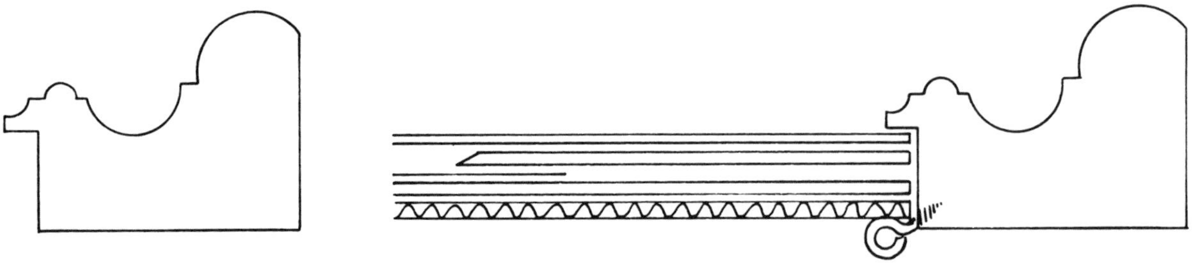

colonial

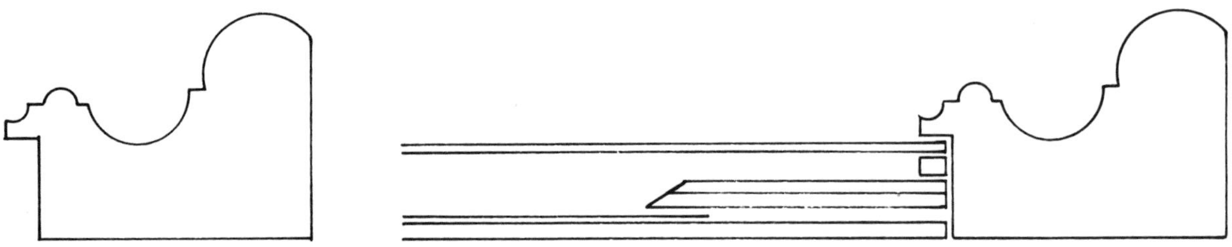

This arched mat was cut to fit the shape of an antique etching. The arch shape was chosen for a practical reason; it was needed to cover the area where the paper had been torn away and left a very irregular edge. A simple matboard backing serves here because of the small size of the piece and the shallow rabbet of the half-round molding. This frame was cut from prefinished gold metal-leaf molding; but the toning was added after the frame was joined. Many picture framers only use prefinished moldings; I prefer frames finished after they are joined because commercially finished moldings have a slickness shared by most mass-produced items. Antique etching, artist unknown.

The box style of framing is so neutral, it might be said to go with any work. Most drawings and prints are complemented by this style; it even works well for color photographs. For black and white photographs I prefer an artificial finish (gray, black, silver). Watercolors and pastels are also flattered by this treatment. The box style makes a fine exhibition frame for mounting a whole show; it makes adequate framing without insisting itself on the viewers. This one is made of basswood and has been given a simple wax finish. The bevel of the mat was colored red to make the color of the woodcut sing. Traditional Japanese woodcut.

This frame is the classic "colonial," one of the most widely used shapes in the framing trade. It is, next to the box style, the most versatile molding shape I know. The colonial fits into almost any decor and complements a wide variety of pictures. Prints, drawings, watercolors, even photographs look fine in this shape, so long as they are of a figurative nature. I would hesitate to use it on abstract, pop, or, in fact, most late-twentieth-century "isms." This example is finished with gold leaf and coated in its cove with orange shellac or "gold" lacquer (clear lacquer tinted to an amber tone). For the example shown, a tan-colored matboard was selected for the base. Soft light tones usually work best for French matting. The lines were drawn with brown drawing ink, the wash was done in watercolor, and the small gold line is a $3/32''$ polyester self-adhesive tape.

Easel-backs work best on frames with low profiles. They are not very successful with box-style frames. Of course, there are many materials other than red velvet that might be used to cover easel-backs. Any fabric you like—imitation leather, decorative papers, or vinyl wall coverings—are suitable materials. Your choice will depend on the finish of the frame and the feeling you are trying to convey. Easel-backed frames are associated almost exclusively with photographs. Miniature paintings, drawings, or prints are often displayed on small tabletop easels but not in easel-backed frames. Sepia photograph of the author's mother.

PUTTING IT ALL TOGETHER

distressed "J"

CROSS SECTION

box

broad flat

floating molding

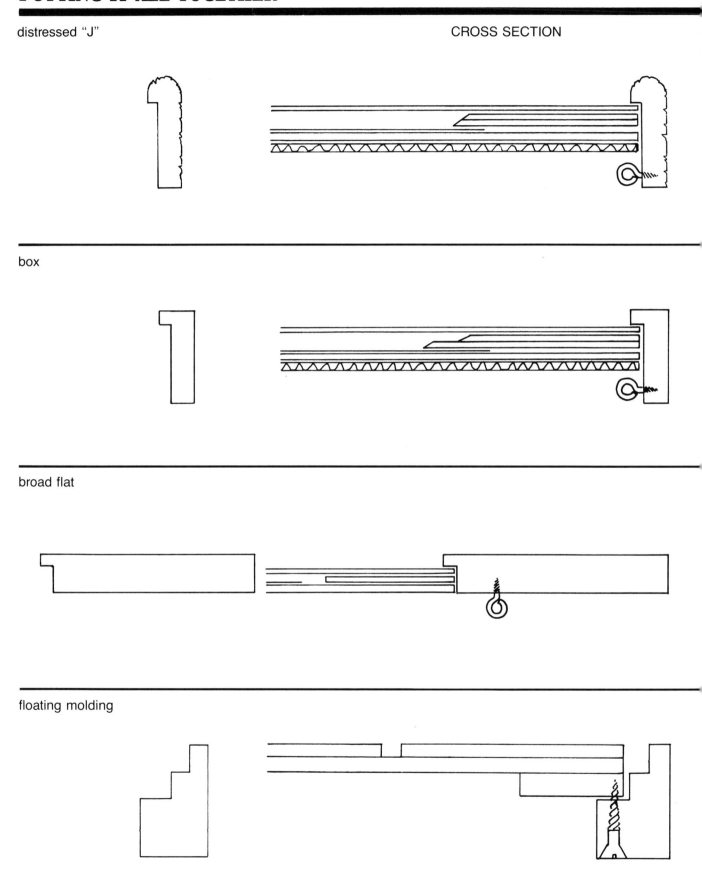

Because the image in this piece is stark and boldly black, I felt the black accent was very appropriate. I have further pushed the black-white contrast by using a black undermat, which adds a dramatic touch to a matted piece. Simple black frames and plain mats are always a safe choice for black and white photographs. I would not use this type of matting on a delicate pencil drawing.

Woodcut, Nickolas Sperakis.

Silk mats and classic gold frames, such as this "J" molding, are almost sure to complement anything. They are such a happy combination that little can be said against their use. They are especially good for small, delicate, and subtly colored works. Perhaps the combination is a little precious for a Käthe Kollwitz, a Van Gogh, or a de Kooning, but I certainly would use it on an Indian miniature, or even a drawing by Matisse. It would also look good on a drawing by Ingres but perhaps not on an Edvard Munch. The nature of the materials used here is complementary to delicate, refined, and deliciously colored things, not strong or brutal works. Intaglio etching, Reuben Kadish.

This flat mat-style frame has been used with a white linen mat inside it to act as a breathing area around the picture. Since the artist has boldly decorated the frame, the calm of the mat is needed here. The painting was done on paper and has been mounted on Masonite. The thickness of the linen mat prevents the picture from touching the glass. This is a necessary precaution in this case because the piece is composed of several different media, which in combination can cause difficulties if adjacent to glass.

Mixed media painting, Rex Clawson.

This floating style, with or without a mat, is often suitable for abstract works where it is desirable to not overlap the edge. However, it is not good when glass is needed, because there is no place to add a retainer. The exposed linen mat, although very handsome, could become a problem in the future because exposure to the elements will eventually soil it. Oil on paper, Budd Hopkins.

PUTTING IT ALL TOGETHER

silver section   CROSS SECTION

shadow box molding

swan

ornamental molding

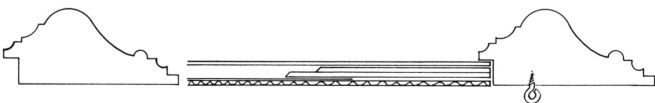

This gold-anodized, aluminum-section frame is used here with two sheets of glass and a wooden filler strip to create the no-mat look. The small wooden strips inserted in the rabbet are painted black, which adds a nice accent to the framing. The effect is airy and spacious. Because of the necessity of hanging this frame by the molding itself, it's not wise to use this treatment on large pieces. In addition the thickness of the wood strips is critical. The strips must be thin enough to allow the taped edges of the glass to enter the rabbet, but thick enough to keep the whole arrangement from shifting. Oil on paper, Don Kunz.

This three-dimensional, crushed beer can demands the depth of the shadow-box frame. Because the can is very colorful, the separation strips were painted with bright red lacquer to complement the bright blue of the can. I finished this frame in aluminum leaf to reflect the shiny quality of the aluminum can itself. It was left untoned, but the gouache quality seemed just right for the subject. Since the objects framed in shadow boxes are rarely art, they provide a field day for the imagination by allowing you to make decorative and playful combinations.

This is an alternate type of shadow-box frame suitable for housing three-dimensional objects, in this case a smashed soy sauce can. Although the framing of a soy sauce can may strike some as an odd subject for framing, it's my contention that any object, properly framed, can be made into a thing of value and beauty. In this example, the space needed for the object is created by the depth of a second frame. This device is similar to separation strips but has the added advantage of presenting the more complex face of a pyramid-style molding. Gold metal-leaf was used to finish the face of the pyramid molding; the backing board is covered with plush red velvet; and the outer frame is lacquered with satin black finish. The O'Keeffe-style outer frame envelopes the inner pyramid frame.

Ordinarily, very simple frames, such as section frames, and mats are suitable for framing photographs, but this unusual view of the head of the Statue of Liberty seemed to call for a special treatment. To reflect the sculptural quality of the subject, I chose a molding with a rolling curve and a few grooves and ridges. Then I painted the frame and toned it to relate to the verdigris coloring of the statue itself. To complement the more complex molding, a double mat seemed to be in order: white under off-white, with the bevel of the top mat painted the green from the frame.
Photograph, Head of the Statue of Liberty, Jerzy Koss.

PUTTING IT ALL TOGETHER

small colonial

"J"

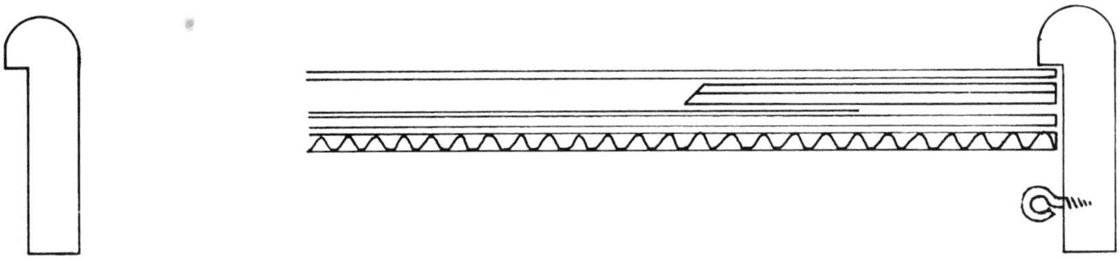

O'Keeffe

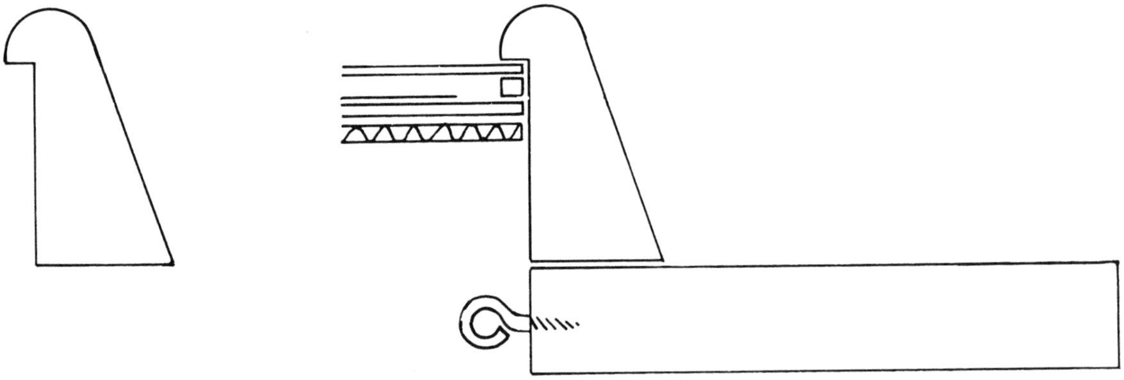

"J"

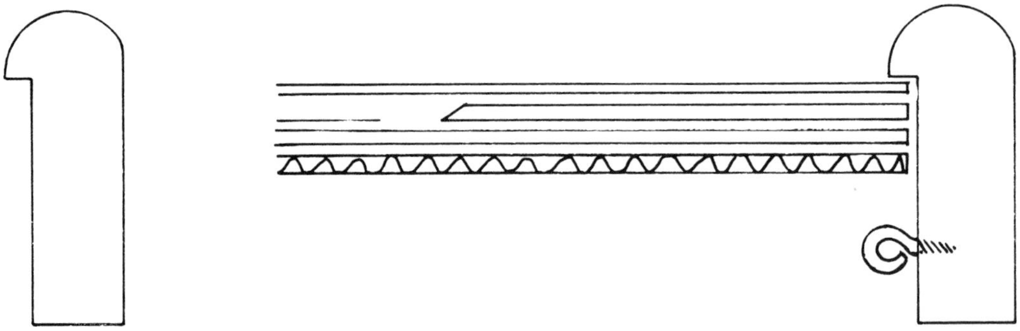

The "J" molding suits this calligraphy very well. Since the piece has some real gold in it, the use of metal leaf for the frame seemed a less than perfect choice. Instead, I decided to finish the frame with aluminum leaf and coat it with orange shellac to give it a gold tone, a technique known as silver-gilt. I also applied a regular oil toning over this, which made the frame a little more golden but still of a higher key than if I had used metal leaf. The bevel of the undermat was gilded with real gold and the top mat was covered in silk. This same combination looks very good on small oriental art works, Persian or Indian miniatures, or other precious works.

Calligraphy, Paul LaPlaca.

This is a small version of the colonial shape molding. Because of the gold lines in the glass mat, a frame of antique gold metal-leaf seemed the appropriate accent. This type of mat is used for antique prints, usually lithographs, but you could give it an updated look by using other mat colors or perhaps combining it with metal-section frames.

This famous rolled slant-back molding, known as the O'Keeffe molding, was my first choice for the top molding of this platform-style frame. The art, a lithograph by Siqueiros, called for a bold, rather heavy treatment. The total effect is dramatic and suitable because this type of frame was popular at the time the print was made. The top molding was finished in satiny black lacquer and mounted on an oak flat frame stained a medium walnut. There is no mat, but the lithograph is hinged with linen tape to a piece of cream-colored museum board. The cream color was chosen to harmonize with the paper of the piece, which had darkened from a previous exposure to an acid-coated backing board.

Lithography, David Siqueriros.

For this delicate pencil drawing, I chose a cherry wood "J" molding. The natural color of the wood relates well to the tones in the paper, which has some discoloration caused by the use of rubber cement. After the drawing had been removed from its original mounting, it was hung from loops of lightweight tape on a piece of cream-colored museum board. The tan matboard mat that surrounds the piece is also an effective solution for harmonizing with the brownish tones of the paper. Drawing, Reuben Kadish.

PUTTING IT ALL TOGETHER

double-sided molding

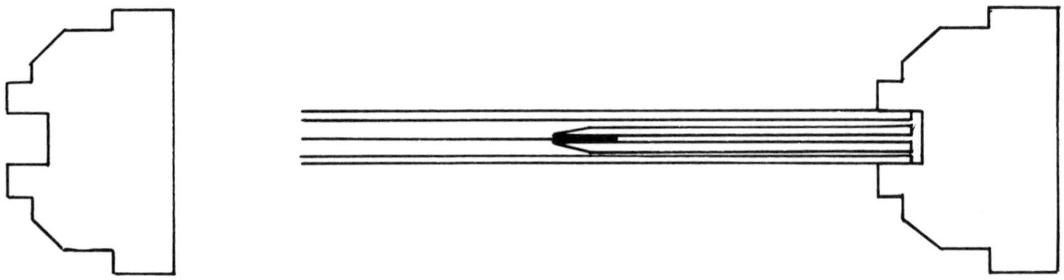

silver section

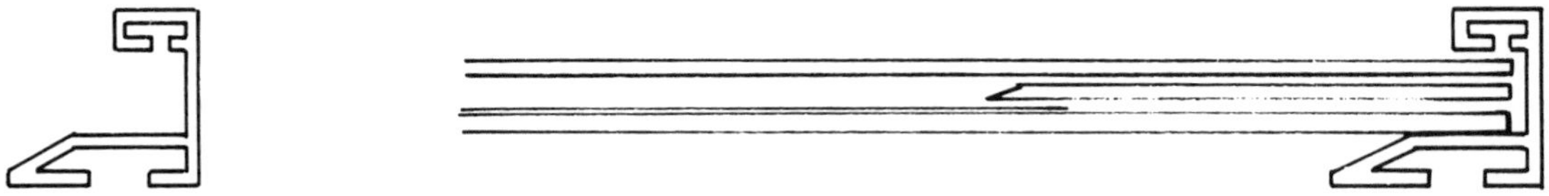

black section

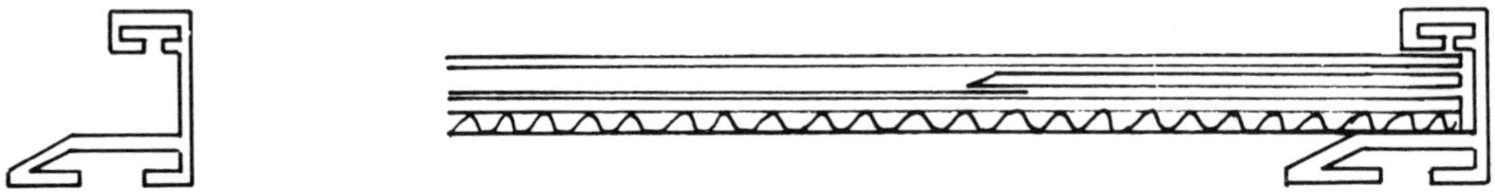

"J"

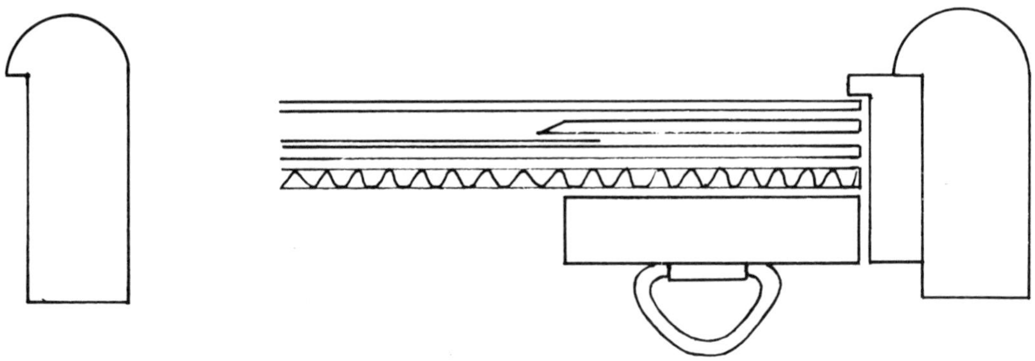

I made this unique molding on the table saw for a double-sided frame. It is made of oak and stained a dark walnut color, a rich coloring and material that relates well to the art—a page from an eighteenth-century Bible. The page was mounted between two tan mats with black bevels and sandwiched between two sheets of glass. This creates a framed object designed to be casually displayed on a coffee table.

This silver (polished aluminum) section frame demonstrates how a conventional standard-size frame can be adapted for a photograph. These frames can be turned horizontally and vertically depending upon the orientation of the photograph. Or, as shown here, they can be left in the vertical position surrounded by a very wide mat, which makes a very handsome framing device. This photograph—a skyline view of Manhattan with ship and bird—is framed by a simple white folder mat and is held in the frame by spring clips. Photograph, Jerzy Koss.

This black section frame creates a thin, dark edge for this calligraphic map of the Sistine Chapel ceiling. The advantage of using a section frame is that it presents the smallest possible face, reading as just a line, which is just the accent this piece needed. Wooden frames can't be made this narrow because they require more hardware at the corner joints. Section frames come in a variety of colors or can be spray-painted with acrylic lacquers. For some work, such as a brightly colored poster, you might want a really lively color to complement the art. Calligraphy, Paul LaPlaca.

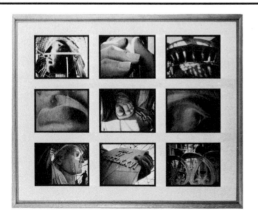

This large piece is composed of nine 8″ × 10″ (20.3 × 25.4 cm) photographs. It is double matted with a black undermat, a design element that adds drama to the arrangement. The frame is a heavy "J" molding of natural wax-finished oak with a painted box liner. Because of its size, the frame required a retainer, although the entire arrangement was made within the limits of a standard-size matboard. If the black undermat hadn't been used here, more space would be needed around the photographs—which would have put the entire piece into an oversize category. With the positive stopping action of the black edges, the denser arrangement was made quite successful. Nine photographs, Jerzy Koss.

PUTTING IT ALL TOGETHER

box

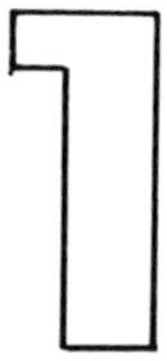

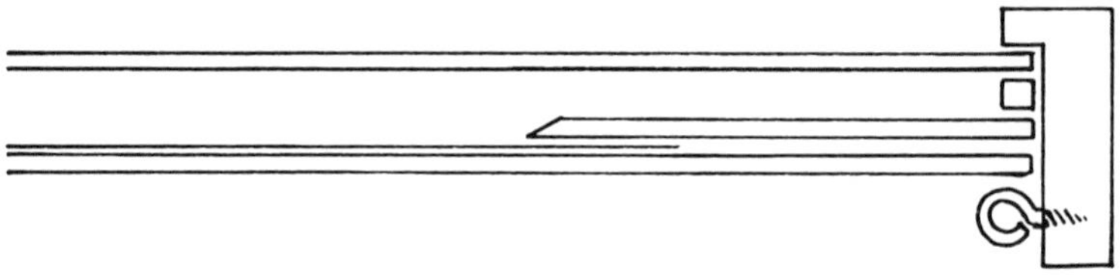

distressed broad bevel

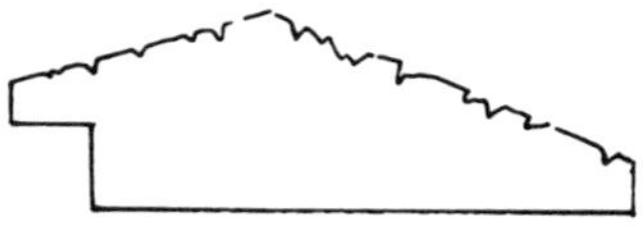

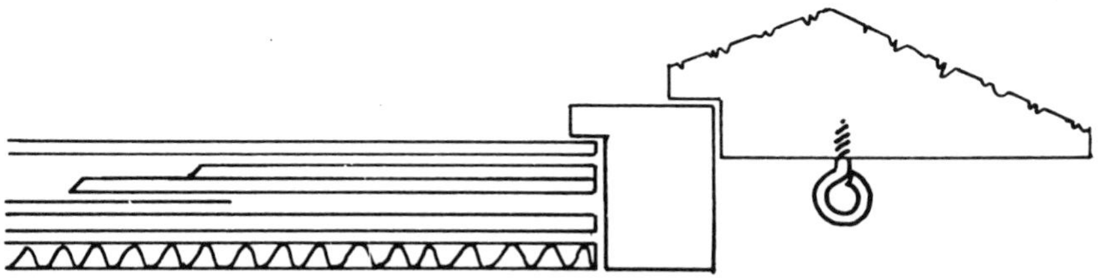

swan

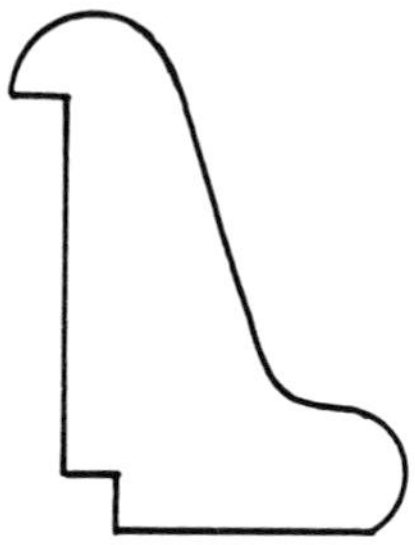

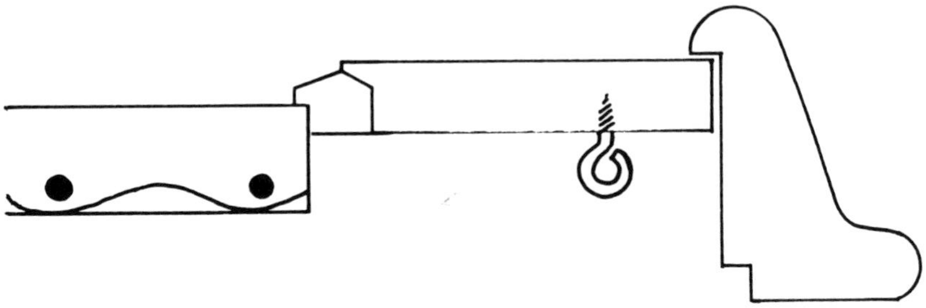

broad flat

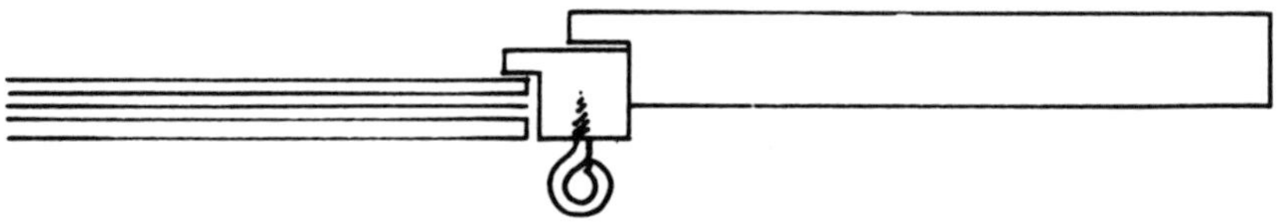

Because this is a simple life study drawn on newsprint, it does not call for a grand framing treatment. A straightforward box style and plain folder mat do the job very well. The mat is not excessively wide, but wide enough to keep the piece to a manageable size. Because newsprint will darken in time, a tan mat was used so as not to call attention to the brown tone. To extend its otherwise short life, the drawing was mounted on chipboard.

Sanquine chalk drawing, Marco Del Rios.

A driftwood frame with a ½" (1.27 cm) white liner is used here with a double mat of pastel green and off white to accent the colors of the sea. The basic gray wash of the driftwood finish was flecked with tones taken from the picture. Ordinarily I never use more than a ¼" (.64 cm) exposure for the undermat, but in this case I felt that the painting needed a wider band. This liner adds life to the soft, muted look of the driftwood. Frames of this sort often look best on outdoor images. Watercolor, Ferdinand Petrie.

This loosely painted landscape done on canvas is framed in a mat style without glass. (Glass should not cover canvas.) The mat is made of basswood and is covered with natural wheat-colored linen. The outer frame is a graceful swan shape made of wormy chestnut and stained a dark walnut. The mat style works well for many subjects, and, by simple variations of finish, it can be made to fit into almost any decor. For example, this same mat style handled more elegantly with silk instead of linen and gilt instead of stain could work successfully for more formal pieces, such as a realistic portrait or a still life. Oil painting, Tom Sullivan.

The mat-style frame is very complementary to contemporary graphics and drawings. Because there are no miter joints and the finish is white lacquer tinted with japan colors, this frame can be expected to hold up for many years. This type of frame usually looks best with a smooth paint job, preferably spray painted. It can also be covered with fabric as long as the edges and corners are handled very carefully. Here, a soft green mat finish was chosen for the mat; the insert is ivory. Silk screen, Corita Kent.

MAKING
A FRAME

To make your own frames, you will need a few tools. First of all you will need a means for cutting the miters. Miter joints are the only type of joints suitable for picture frames. (For strainers, lap-joints are stronger and possible because there is no rabbet.) The tool used for making miters on a small scale is the steel miter box. The small wooden miter boxes that carpenters often use to make trim moldings are not satisfactory. Although it is possible to make a few frames using the wooden miter box, it soon wears out and becomes inaccurate. You can buy a good miter box for about sixty dollars. It should have the capability of making a 45° cut from either the right or the left and a 90° cut in the middle. The better boxes adjust to any angle from 45° to 90°.

Miter boxes come furnished with a saw called a "back saw." It is called a back saw because of the thick top edge that runs along its back. The purpose of this edge is to stiffen the saw and to act as a stop for the depth of cut, so that the teeth never touch the miter box. Unlike ordinary handsaws that are tapered, the back saw is straight and uniform in width. Back saws come with various teeth, but those sold with a miter box are fine-toothed crosscut saws; they are usually referred to as miter saws.

You will also need a vise for joining the frame, or at least some type of corner clamps. Other necessary items include an awl to make starter holes for nails and screw eyes, a hammer for joining, and a nail set to punch the brads slightly under the surface. The hammer should be of the claw type and weigh no more than a pound. Hammers that are sixteen ounces or more are too large to be the best tools for joining. For the most part you will be driving tiny wire brads or small finishing nails. In addition you'll be needing an upholsterer's tack hammer for the fitting operation, but a tack hammer is not good as a joining hammer; the claw hammer is better because its slightly rounded face is less likely to mar the molding. A pair of wire cutters of the type called "diagonals" is very useful for extracting nails as well as cutting wire; and ordinary gas pliers are helpful for driving in screw eyes.

CUTTING AND JOINING

With the saw set to the left side of the miter box, place the molding against the back wall of the miter box and hold it firmly in place with the left hand. The rabbet should be facing you. Lower the saw and make your first cut. Now, placing your rule at the cut edge, measure along the back of the rabbet to the length you want and make a mark with the pencil. Always use a soft pencil in frame making, never a ballpoint or marker; these can make stains that can't be removed later. At this point, keep in mind the need for "allowance," a term used to indicate the extra length given to the molding pieces in order to accommodate the glass, mat, and backing. If you buy a ready-made frame marked 16″ × 20″ (40.64 × 50.8 cm) and measure it within the rabbet of the frame, you will find that it actually measures something like 16⅛″ × 20⅛″ (40.96 × 51.15 cm). It is customary to give ⅛″ (.32 cm) allowance to frames that are

to receive glass and mat. The allowance for canvas frames is often even more; because of the out-of-square nature of the pieces being framed, a ¼″ (.64 cm) allowance is typical.

Make your mark on the back of the rabbet to include the allowance. Pass the molding under the saw until the mark has more than cleared the right-hand 45° slot in the miter box—this will allow for the making of the miter cut on that end (but don't make it now because that would entail shifting the saw to the other side). Then make all your beginning cuts, being sure to leave enough molding to make the other miter cut. Move the saw to the other side and cut all the opposite ends. For these cuts you will be holding the molding against the back wall with your right hand and using the saw with your left. Some types of molding, such as the broader flats, can be cut all from the same side because they can be turned upside down; but moldings that have shaped faces must be cut from both saw positions.

Joining is the next step. The person who does this in a commercial shop is known as a joiner and he or she must be very fast. There are special vises for holding the moldings at a right angle and special stapling tools. Here, I am dealing with the very simplest methods, methods you can use in your own work space. If you are right-handed, the right end of each molding strip (with the rabbet facing you) will be the one which will be nailed. Nails will be easier to start if you make beginning holes with the point of an awl. If the molding is hardwood, such as, oak, maple, or walnut, it will be necessary to drill holes; otherwise, the nailing will not only be difficult, it will split the molding. The holes are drilled only through the right-hand end, not into the piece into which you are nailing. The nail will be going into the end-grain condition of that piece; hence, it will not cause splitting.

Make a habit of always doing an operation in the same order; this will prevent mistakes. For instance, I always put the long piece of molding into the vise first and then join the short piece to it; then I repeat the operation, putting the other long piece in the vise and joining the other short piece to it. This leaves me with two L-shapes, which I then join together to make the frame. If you work randomly and do not follow a pattern, you will probably discover that you have made a corner that does not meet and make a frame with the other corner, a mistake that is very disconcerting the first time it happens.

Let us then (following correct procedure) put the long piece of molding in the vise with the mitered end just free of the jaws. The faces of the jaws should be made smooth and somewhat resilient. You can cover them with leather (an old belt) or use cardboard such as double-thick matboard or ⅛″ (.32 cm) chipboard; these can be attached with contact cement or simply taped to the vise faced with masking tape. As you nail, the molding must be locked securely into the vise to prevent movement. For most moldings the nailing will be done with two or three wire brads in each corner. The size of the brads will depend on the width of molding used; the larger the molding the larger the brad required. Molding sizes from ½″ (1.27 cm) to 1″ (2.54 cm) need only ¾″ (1.91 cm) number 18 brads. Moldings larger than 1″ (2.54 cm) may be held by 1″ (2.54 cm) or 1¼″ (3.18 cm) number 16 wire brads. Think of the brads as a kind of clamping device because it's really the glue that holds the corner securely. The brads pull the pieces of molding together and keep them in place until the glue sets.

You can choose to make your frames without nailing if you like. This simply means you will need at least four corner clamps. The clamped frame is best left in the clamps at least two hours, so this method slows down production time. If you choose the gluing method, there is a strengthening device called a "feather spline" that adds a finished touch to hardwood frames.

To make a feather spline, two or three saw cuts are run into the outside corner at a right angle to the miter. These are then filled with slivers of hardwood and glue. A contrasting color is very effective, such as walnut splines in a maple frame. These slivers are cut and sanded to match the surface of the frame, thus creating small triangles that tie the corner together. The grain of the splines should run across the miter, of course.

But getting back to the nailing method: place one long piece of the molding in the vise with the rabbet facing away from you and the lip of the rabbet resting on the top of the jaws. Here, you are clamping the frame in a horizontal condition, with just the miter cut projecting from the jaws. The adjacent short side is now put into place and held by the left hand, with hand and wrist resting on the vise to steady the molding. Now insert the first nail into the top hole. The holes should be the same size as the nail, the idea being that the nail should slip easily through the first piece of molding and penetrate the second piece into which it's driven, thus pulling the joint together in a clamplike fashion. A small tip which will prove useful is to start the first nail with the molding at least 1/16″ (.16 cm) back of its true position. The molding has a tendency to slide forward as you drive in the nails, so take advantage of this fact to help you lock the corner. Drive the first nail in until it is flush with the molding surface, then strike it again (and perhaps again) until the molding is in the proper position. This will make a kind of hook out of the first nail and create a firm tight joint. Be sure the molding is in the proper place with this first nail, as it will not slide with the second or third.

Of course, at this stage it is presumed you have already applied glue to the joint before nailing. The best practice is to precoat the ends of all the pieces with a thin coat of glue and let them dry five minutes or more, then apply glue to one side and nail the joint. This assures a good tight joint. The end-grain condition of the miter joint absorbs glue, readily leaving the joint "glue starved" if it is not double-coated.

After creating the two L-shapes, join them to make a finished frame. If the frame is of considerable size—say over 16″ × 20″ (40.64 × 50.8 cm)—it may be necessary to provide additional support to the diagonal corner. Depending on the position of your vise, this can be accomplished by making blocks or boxes to stand on the table; I have used a kind of wedge device, a 10″ (25.4 cm) tall block with a sloping surface so that the varying depths of moldings can be accommodated. With the rabbet resting on the vise lip, the bottom of the frame becomes the point that needs support, varying in its height with each molding. I have found that if the frame is quite large so the diagonal corner juts out off the table, a floor stand with adjustable height is very useful. Of course, a person who is willing to stand there for you and hold the molding also works very well, but barring this happy circumstance, a satisfactory stand can be made from an adjustable music stand whose sheet music holder has been replaced by a block of wood. I have also used one leg of an oak drawing table, to which I had added a block of wood at the top and four casters at the bottom for this purpose. You could also design and build your own stand if you have the inclination.

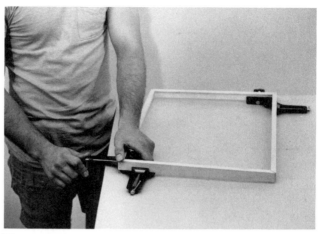

The use of corner clamps provides an alternate method for joining. This method requires more time but is easier for unskilled hands.

As each corner is nailed and the frame is still held in the vise, use a 1/32″ nail set to punch the heads of the brads below the surface of the wood. After the nailing is done, set the frame aside for at least two hours so that the glue can dry. I am assuming you are using some standard carpenter's glue (such as Elmer's, Tite-Bond, Franklin's) or one of the many other yellowish alaphatic resin glues on the market. The polyvinyl white glues are also good, though they are more flexible and cannot be sanded as easily. The traditional glue for all woodworking purposes is animal, or hoof and hide, glue. Its disadvantage is that it must be kept hot in a double-jacketed glue pot and is not significantly better than the standard glues just mentioned. The one advantage to animal glue, however, is that it sticks immediately.

Other glues do not work so well, such as Duco or Testors, or any of the other acrylic lacquer cements or so-called "airplane" glues. The hot glues used in hot-glue guns are not very good either. These glues are sometimes used commercially but usually on ready-made "dime-store" frames. There are also a number of special glues that are used in combination with stapling tools to join commercial frames, but they are not needed for the handmade frame.

After you have properly joined the frame, set it aside to dry for at least two hours before continuing. If you find nailing in the vise difficult, you might try joining with the corner clamps. This method requires very little technique and gives good results although it has the disadvantage of being rather slow. When working with the clamps, you may find it easier if you think of the inside edge of the clamp as the glass part of a frame. You should push both pieces of the molding tight against the inner surface and make them match as you would like them to be in the frame. Then tighten one side of the clamp. I am assuming here that you have precoated the miters with glue. Now remove one piece of molding and coat it again with glue. Return it to its previous place and tighten the other side of the clamp. Now make another L using another clamp. If you have two more clamps, you may then proceed to join the two L-shapes as in the nailing method; if not, let these two dry for two hours or so. Then remove them from the clamps and proceed to join them using the same two clamps—a process which, of course, takes some time. To expedite matters you may nail the corner in the clamp and remove the clamp and proceed.

MAKING A FRAME

1 Cut the molding to size using a steel miter box.

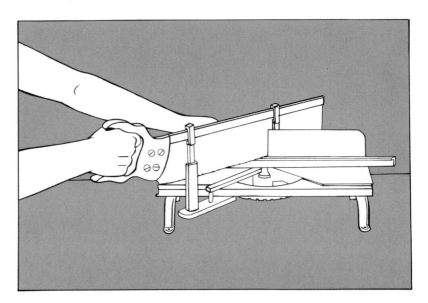

2 Join the frame together with brads and glue. While drawing in the brads, brace your hand on the vise to steady the frame.

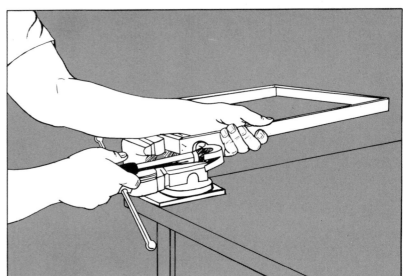

3 With the molding still held in the vise, set the nails slightly under the surface with a 1/32" nail set.

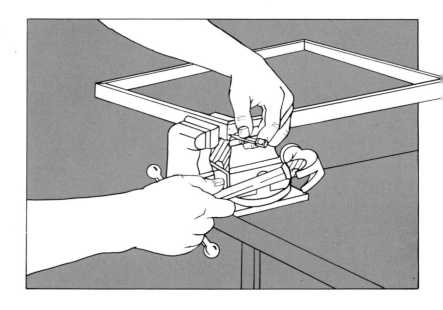

FINISHING

The first step in any finish is to stuff the nail holes and any other discrepancies in the joints or molding with a putty. I suggest Durham's water putty, which is a form of plaster of Paris. It sets in ten minutes, so it must be mixed in small quantities. It is tinted with dry color to approximate the look of "wood," which turns out to be rather like the color called "flesh" in oil paints. However, this solution is better than leaving the holes plain white; and in some cases the color is close enough to wood to actually work. In other instances the putty may require a little touching-up. The good thing about water putty is its ability to fill the hole. Wood putty is basically plaster, therefore it expands when it sets and forces itself against the sides of the hole. Many other materials, such as the various forms of "plastic wood," tend to shrink when they dry and will eventually fall out. Some framers use the types of vinyl putty used in house repair; the brand Dap is an example. Other framers still rely on the old-fashioned linseed oil putty used to glaze windows.

The next step is sanding. I suggest 120 aluminum oxide production sandpaper or something very close to it. This paper gives a somewhat toothy surface that's a perfect surface for either gesso or casein paint. If you plan to stain the frame, you might follow the original sanding with 220 sandpaper.

In general, I don't think staining is a good idea. If you are after a "wood" look, the best thing to do is to use a handsome wood for the molding. Cherry, walnut, oak, maple, or birch are examples; and these are best finished in a very simple way—by waxing or oiling. A wax finish is applied with a thinned-down coat of shellac (one-third alcohol to two-thirds shellac) to the wood, which is then left to dry for at least two hours. Then, using double-aught (double 00) steel wool, rub the surface down to a very smooth condition and apply paste wax. Butcher's Bowling Alley is an example of a very good paste wax. Twenty minutes after you apply it, you can buff the finish to a slight sheen and it's done.

Applying an oil finish is also simple. Both Watco and Gillespie's tung oil are good choices. Or, you can simply make a mix that is half boiled linseed oil and half turpentine. Apply this mixture and let it set or penetrate about twenty minutes; then wipe it to remove the excess oil and let it dry overnight. If the finish is not glossy or "high" enough, repeat the process. Oil brings out the natural beauty and grain of the wood. An oil finish can also be waxed if desired.

I have already stated that I don't recommend staining. I feel this way because staining, except when done by expert hands, very often looks "fake." For example, if you take a basswood molding and try to make it look like walnut, the results look like a mistake. On the other hand, you might succeed with a birch molding because its grain and texture are more like walnut. By the way, basswood is the most commonly used wood in the framing trade.

If you decide to use stained finishes anyway, I can give you a few hints. First of all, don't go out and buy "stains;" you can make any kind of stain you need by simply diluting oil color with turpentine. For instance, you can duplicate the effect of walnut stain by simply mixing burnt umber oil color with a little turpentine (the amount of turpentine is dependent on the lightness or darkness desired). The color base for an oak stain is basically raw sienna; and maple is raw sienna with a touch of burnt sienna.

After you have applied the stain solution with a brush or rag, wipe it to the intensity you desire. When it is thoroughly dry (the next day), coat the surface with a thinned-down shellac, by which I mean one-third alcohol to two-thirds shellac. Later, when gilded finishes are discussed, I will go over the means of making this essential staining more rich and more convincing by the addition of "glazing." Otherwise, if this look satisfies you, rub it down lightly with steel wool and apply paste wax. It is also possible to build quite a good look to these finishes by adding another glaze. You can apply additional glazes by separating each layer with shellac. Since shellac dissolves only in alcohol and there is no alcohol in any of the glazings, there is no problem in adding another layer. Simply staining and waxing often results in a rather "cheap" look; by giving the wood a little more attention, what is called a "tickled" finish is created, which can result in some very beautiful effects. My advice here is never to be discouraged by a seemingly poor result; you can always alter it. To impart depth and richness, it's best to stain a shade lighter than you desire, then seal it with shellac, and glaze it darker.

Another type of finish is the plain "painted" one, which is most often accomplished with spraying techniques or by brushing on japan colors. The spray approach can be handled on a small scale with spray cans. Krylon makes a good flat white, a very nice velvety black called "High Heat," and a sandable gray primer. All three of these spray can finishes must be done in several stages. First, you should wipe the dust from the frame. Then, lay the frame in a horizontal position on two sticks resting on paper either outdoors or near a window (preferably with a fan), because good ventilation is a must. Start spraying at the near edge, on the back of the frame and the top, then go across and spray the inner lip edge and the top of the opposite side. To turn the frame easily a quarter turn at a time without getting paint on your hands, reach inside the rabbet with both hands. Now spray the near edge again and the inner lip and top of the opposite side. This technique of always spraying away from you keeps the "dust" of the lacquer from settling on the fresh paint. When you have turned the frame two more times, you will have made a careful coating of the entire surface of the frame.

Let this spray coating dry. Then rub gently with double-aught steel wool, a process that smoothes out the roughness and irregularities of the surface. Clean the surface by wiping with a soft cloth and spray again in the same manner. For the most constant lighting conditions, I favor standing in the same place and rotating the frame. If you try to move around the frame, the lighting will invariably change, and it becomes difficult to judge the result. In fact, I suggest this approach when doing any of the finishes, even though it may require three coats and rubbing with steel wool between each.

There are problems encountered in spray painting. If you move too close with the spray can or hold it too long in one spot, sags and runs can result. If this happens, don't try to correct these right away; wait until they have dried. Then, using a small piece of wet or dry 400 or 600 sandpaper (the black kind), dip the paper into a little benzine (not benzene, which is toxic and should not be used) and sand the surface lightly. The benzine will not quite dissolve the lacquer, but will soften it enough to smooth it out for the next spraying.

These same techniques apply to spraying with industrial lacquer. If you have an airbrush or spraying system, you will be able to apply a lacquer finish. The basic lacquer I use is an industrial white semigloss or satin finish, which is available from industrial paint suppliers. It's the same paint used to finish refrigerators and cars. The best thing about using lacquers as opposed to spray cans is that you can create virtually any color you want. Notice the white liner and the soft gray green frame used for the print by Corita Kent on page 00. The frame's color was created by adding japan color to the basic white lacquer, a little raw sienna, a little raw umber, and a touch of chrome green. When you mix colors like this, add the color to a small amount of white lacquer in a can or jar. Mix the colors with a brush, such as a small artist's fitch, until the color is blended. Then, add the lacquer thinner to make a sprayable mixture. This method gives you complete control over the medium. If you want the color a little paler, add white lacquer, or if you want the color cast a little bit more blue, all you need to do is add a little more blue. According to paint suppliers, japan colors are desirable in this regard, but oil colors are not. However, I have found that a good grade of oil color (that is, pigment which is not swimming in oil) works, but you should be careful to add the oil color to the full-strength white lacquer and then dilute it with thinner—otherwise there will be separation.

Another type of painted finish I favor is to choose a color that harmonizes with the picture. It should be a soft shade and in a higher key than you expect the finished frame to be. This can be lacquer tinted with japan color or oil color. If you do not have spraying facilities, then use alkyd flat white and tint it with oil colors. A typical example would be tan or pale olive green. The next step is to apply a toning color over the first coat. If you do use alkyd paint it will be necessary to isolate the first coat with shellac before applying the toning color. The second coat should be in the same color range as the first but several shades darker. The toning color should be a mixture of oil color with turpentine and a little boiled linseed oil. Apply it with a brush to liberally cover the frame; then using a soft cloth, gently wipe off the excess to distribute it as evenly as you can. Using the ends of the bristles of a large, soft, dry brush, stipple the entire surface leaving an even glaze. The center of large areas may be wiped again with cheesecloth or a similar soft cloth if desired. This will produce a shaded effect.

Distressing is another type of finish; it means scratching and injuring the frame to give it the look of age. I use a variety of scratching, beating, and puncturing tools for achieving this effect. The idea is to give the impression that the molding has been around for a long time. Some call this technique antiquing, but others find that term offensive or at least inaccurate. Some say that the term antiquing applies only to the glazing and rottenstoning. Whatever the view, the process consists of using such tools as an awl or other pointed instrument to scratch and to punch "worm" holes. The standard "church key," or bottle opener, is ideal for scratching molding. Its pointed end used to puncture holes into canned goods gives an uneven line according to varying pressure; and it is quite easy to guide it in random paths along the top and sides of the frame. The tack hammer is useful for striking gentle blows here and there. You can use both the face and the side of the hammer. Some people even use chains and flail away at their frames, but the hammer is enough for me.

Distressing techniques are usually applied to the frame in its raw state, similar to the preparation of the molding to make a "driftwood" effect. Sometimes it is done to more or

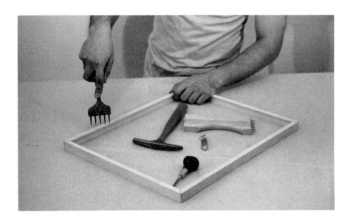

If you want driftwood or barn-siding effects, you will need to distress the surface of the wood. Distressing is sometimes used in combination with gilding to create texture and the effects of age.

less finished frames in order to dislodge pieces of gesso and to scratch gold leaf (steel wool or coarse sandpaper is good for this). However, when distressing is done to a finished frame, the damage just looks too new. This effect can be cured by washing the new frame with dirty turpentine, by which I mean turpentine in which a brush or two have been cleaned of umbers and/or black. Then brush the turpentine on, wipe it off, and dust with rottenstone. Rottenstone by the way is packaged dust and is available wherever dry colors are sold (hardware or paint stores). It is usually used as a polishing agent, but in framing it's used to imitate the look of dust; it achieves this look by sticking to the residue of color in the dirty turpentine and by giving a more realistic "aged" look to the distressed surface. To make a "driftwood" effect, scratch the molding as soon as the frame is joined. A lot of scratching is necessary, followed by a loose sandpapering with very coarse sandpaper or dragging with a wood rasp. This creates a texture that will "grab" subsequent glazings. You can even punch a few holes here and there but don't overdo it.

Next, apply a dark stain, such as umber, in either oil or japan color, and dissolve it in turpentine. Let this coating dry and seal it with shellac. The shellac should be cut about one-third with alcohol in order to promote drying and to prevent a gummy buildup. When the shellac has dried, apply a glaze of gray casein. This glaze is made by mixing a little black and a little umber casein colors into some white casein. If casein colors are not available locally you can get by with latex or acrylic housepaints and universal tinting colors, though both these are not as good and are more difficult to control. Thin this mixture with water and apply with a brush. Using a damp cloth, immediately wipe the surface and continue wiping until you have left an evenly distributed thin coating. This coating will become more opaque as it dries. After it dries, use coarse steel wool (no. 3) to scratch the surface and reveal some of the brown beneath. In more elaborate forms of this finish, you can build up a smattering of drybrush markings underneath, using colors that relate to the painting being framed; but this is generally done on more massive frames, such as those used for oils and other paintings on panels or canvas.

If you want to introduce color variety into your finish, use alkyd white housepaint (flat) as a base and tint it to match the various colors in the painting. Mix a small puddle of white on your palette, and add a little raw sienna into it or whatever color you want to pick up. With a stiff artist's fitch brush of about 1" (2.54 cm), pick up a little of the color and whisk it across a newspaper. When you see that you are getting a nice drybrush effect, apply these marks to the frame; if necessary recharge and apply again. Then, mix another color and repeat the process. Try hitting in between spots so that your drybrushed colors don't mix. These brushstrokes are being applied to the shellac coating that isolates the dark stain.

When you have finished applying the drybrush brushstrokes, let the paint dry overnight. Then shellac again; and when that is dry proceed to apply a gray casein glaze. Rub the casein glaze down with steel wool. It's often a good idea at this point to also apply a dirty turpentine wash and rottenstone dusting. Even a few flecks applied with toothbrush and a stick help. Then, work the surface until it says to you, "I am driftwood." If things don't seem to go right, let the coating dry overnight and strike it down with coarse sandpaper the next day, then shellac again and continue. Remember, there is no such thing as too much—and less is definitely not more.

Driftwood effects often look best on such pieces as seascapes or country landscapes. In general, watercolors are compatible with the distressed look. And some drawings, especially of a traditional sort, look good in this type of frame. For example, chalk drawings and drawings that are loosely done are appropriate in this context. However, photographs probably would look very odd in this context. Works by artists such as Aubrey Beardsley would look totally alien framed in driftwood. To my eye, Beardsley requires polished black lacquer, and Rubens cries out for antique gold. The seascapes of Winslow Homer might take to driftwood, but the stark, industrial cityscapes of Charles Demuth would not, nor would the rigid geometry of Mondrian. Mondrian would be complemented by semigloss black or white frames—please, no silver! Pop artist Jasper Johns deserves silver (polished aluminum). Abstractionist Robert Motherwell deserves red and black and sometimes a touch of gold. And "combine" artist Robert Rauschenburg perhaps requires no frame at all; or, at the very least, a tiny frame to accent one of the elements in his work.

Thus, the style of the work of art you are framing has everything to do with the type of frame you choose. When I am presented with a work to frame, the first consideration is one of style. If I don't like the work, then it becomes a torment to decide; but if I like it the solution comes freely. Although I have often heard it said that artists don't know how to frame their own work, it just isn't true. Hack artists do not know, perhaps; but real artists have wonderful ideas and solutions. In the 1940s and 1950s American artist John Marin framed his own watercolors and drawings in frames he made and decorated himself. I have always admired him for doing that. Paul Klee is another artist who made his own frames. In the examples shown, two frames have been decorated by the artist. When the frame is done by the artist, I would give him or her complete license in this matter; whatever is produced by this union has typically got to be better than anything someone from the outside could impose.

There's a very simple class of finishes known as antique white, which is actually casein white. This paint comes in a can in paste form and should be diluted with water, but not so much that you could use it for painting. It must retain enough body not to flow and also to be able to hold the

marks of the brushwork. Although this type of finish works best when applied linearly to the full lengths of molding before the frame is assembled, it can be applied to a completed, joined frame if you take special care painting around the corners. If you are applying it to the full-length molding (which typically comes in lengths of 8' to 14'), clamp one end of the molding to the table or place in a vise. (A small portion of the end will, of course, not be usable.) Rest the other end on a stand of equal height. My converted music stand that I use for joining large frames works well. Now with the full length of molding in the air, you can easily apply the finish. Make sure to cover the floor under the molding with papers to catch the drippings. Now apply the diluted casein paint. A good brush for this purpose is a "sash" brush (intended for painting window frames). This brush is round and rather full, and is 1¼" to 1½" (3.17 to 3.81 cm) in diameter. The rather stiff quality of the sash brush's natural black bristles will help give texture.

Using long straight strokes, apply the first coat of casein with care, starting at one end and covering all visible sides of the molding. Then stand the molding aside to dry and repeat on all the lengths you are preparing.

After approximately an hour, the second coat should be applied. Pay special attention to this coating because whatever configuration you leave in the surface of the paint will appear later as pattern after you "antique" the wood. After casein coating the entire length, go back over the surface immediately with the brush, dragging it from one end to the other to create a uniform pattern. You may also find that "stippling" with the ends of the bristles gives a nice textured effect; this is particularly a good solution when the frame is already assembled. In any case, the texturing must be done quickly while the coating of paint is still fresh enough to retain the brushwork. At this point stand the moldings aside to dry completely. So long as you have the ceiling height to accommodate the molding lengths, they simply can be leaned up against the wall.

When the moldings are dry (later the same day is fine), you can proceed to the antiquing step. Antiquing requires the application of dirty turpentine. To do this, place some turpentine (I prefer gum turpentine because it is more pleasant than wood turpentine to work with) in a can and add a little raw umber japan or oil color to it (universal tinting colors may be used but are not as easily controlled). To this mix add just a hint of black. Later you may wish to vary your color and, of course, any color can be used to alter the color of the white. For example, burnt umber gives a more tan effect, raw sienna more ivory, and raw umber with black gives a nice neutral gray. Remember that this mixture is not "paint" but a light stain, so don't overdo the pigment. Dirty turpentine, yes, but not too dirty!

Apply the dirty turpentine with a rag or a ball of cotton wadding. Dip the rag into the turpentine and with the molding back in the painting position, rub the surface quickly and briskly. Be generous with this wetting and rubbing dry. The effect should come out quite even, turning the casein gray. You may immediately follow this step by rubbing it with a no. 3 steel wool pad, which will strike the high points of your texture, leaving little white lines or specks on the gray.

Once the frame is joined, the antique finish requires little work. Ordinary linseed oil putty (the type glaziers use) is good for stuffing the nail holes, and if you are very careful with the joining there should be little or no sanding of the corners. Most commercial framing is done with prefinished molding.

GOLD LEAFING

Many frames require a gilded finish so this is perhaps the most important type of molding finish to learn. In the oval mat section (pages 37 to 43) there is a brief demonstration of the laying of real gold. In this section, I am going to cover the laying of imitation gold or "metal leaf;" this is the "gold leaf" of most picture framing. Of course, real gold is superior to metal leaf both in its lasting qualities and in beauty; but since the price of gold is so high and the labor required to prepare its surface so specialized, the laying of real gold has diminished to a point where it is used by only very fine framers doing museum-quality work. This is a little sad and was not always the case. However, we must all deal with the realities of today.

My intention here is to give you a technique for applying gold leaf that will serve your needs and at the same time won't be difficult to master. This technique is known as oil gilding, which means that the gold is made to adhere to the surface by means of an oil "size" or varnish. Most gold sizes are made of boiled linseed oil and japan dryer. This mixture forms a varnish that dries to a "tack" and then receives the leaf.

In order to understand this process more clearly, let's begin with the surface to which the gold is applied. Since picture frames are usually made of wood, the wood surface must be prepared to the point where a coat of varnish can be applied. Gold leaf needs a primer-sealer of some sort. Shellac mixed with dry color is one possibility. I prefer the casein colors. A mixture of burnt sienna and red will give you a color resembling red bole, which is the all-time favorite of those who lay real gold leaf. Other colors of clay are also used, such as green and yellow ochre and dark blue; but I prefer the red bole. Casein colors are available from suppliers that cater to theater set makers. These colors come in cans and are in paste form. The paste must be diluted with water to a brushable consistency. Don't make the paste too thin. This material serves as both a substitute for gesso and the red clay size.

Apply the casein with a brush and let it dry for about two hours. Use steel wool to smooth the surface and remove any runs. Then wipe the dust away and recoat with casein. When this coat is dry, repeat the steel wooling (no. 1 is good) and coat with thinned shellac. A five-pound cut should be cut to about one-third alcohol to two-thirds shellac. (The cut refers to how many pounds of gum shellac have been dissolved in one gallon of alcohol.) If you get your shellac at a dime store or discount store, it will most probably be already thinned. Two thin coats of shellac provide a good seal for the casein and make it ready to receive the size. The idea here is to apply the varnish to a nonporous surface, so that it will set to a tack—then you can apply the leaf. So, if you are applying the gold leaf to a nonabsorbant surface, such as plastic or metals, this preparation of the surface becomes unnecessary.

In the demonstration shown I am using quick size. Quick size reaches proper tack in one to three hours. Slow size reaches tack in ten to thirteen hours. Specific times cannot be given because the drying of the size is dependent on many variables, such as heat, humidity, and movement of air. Proper precautions should be taken: Don't place the sized frame in direct sunlight. Don't use electric fans to dry the size faster, because the size needs to dry to a tack slowly, and a fan will dry it too quickly. Work in as clean an atmosphere as possible. Always cover your surfaces with paper and make sure your frame rests on sticks so it won't stick to the paper.

Use the size directly from the can—don't shake or stir it. Pour a little size into a clean container and don't return any leftover to the can. Keep the can sealed at all times, and when the level has fallen enough, transfer the contents to a smaller jar or container so that the size won't develop a "skin" so readily. When a film forms on the surface of the size simply peel it back and pour the size from underneath. Remember, don't thin the size; use it straight from the can and make sure to apply a thorough coating. It's a little difficult to see the size on the shellacked surface; the addition of a little chrome yellow oil color will make the size more visible, but this retards the setting time. And once you have moved to another side of the frame, don't go back over areas that have already received the size. After you have applied the size, let the frames dry for an hour, then test for the tack. Testing is done by touching your knuckle to the surface. The knuckle of your middle finger is the usual one I use for testing; it should come away clean and with a slight "ticking" sound. This sound means the size is ready. If it doesn't tick wait a half hour and try again. If you lay the leaf too soon—before the tack is right—you won't have a good job.

The leaf you will most likely be using is metal leaf no. 2½. It is considered by most to be closest in color to double XX gold for surface gilding. Of course, you can also lay real gold using this same size; the difference is the method of handling the leaf. You can also use aluminum leaf for silver or silver-gilt finishes. Metal leaf books contain twenty-five sheets, five-inches square. They can be purchased in individual books or by the pack, which consists of twenty books. The pack is the more economical way to buy; it also comes in a box without tissue between and is used on a commercial scale. Many art-supply stores stock metal leaf, but the best prices are usually found from suppliers to the sign-painting trade.

To facilitate handling the leaf, tear the book in half parallel to its spine, and then carefully tear the spine away as well. When doing very small moldings or portions of moldings, you should tear the leaf into even smaller pieces. I suggest tearing the leaf as opposed to cutting with scissors because the scissors will cause all the tissue pages to stick together, which makes the leaves difficult to handle. Then, holding half a book in one hand, use the other hand to position the leaf on the sized surface. You may find it helpful to press lightly on the tissue to adhere the leaf before discarding the tissue.

After laying in at least one whole side of the frame, go back with a soft brush, such as camel hair or oxhair, and pat the leaf all over. This requires a dual operation of applying and removing. A sort of pat and whisk motion will develop as you get the hang of it. Don't worry at this point about removal of all the little pieces, but do concern yourself with the covering of all the surface. Small pieces may be picked up from the table and attached at this stage; but where there are "holidays" (points missed in painting the size) in the size the leaf will not stick. These spots will then have to be resized. Sometimes a few missed spots are desirable, such as if you are working toward a distressed look.

The next day is the time to come back and rub and polish the leaf with a cotton ball or piece of velvet to remove all the little pieces of gold, or skewings. There is a practice called backbrushing that's done to emphasize the leafed effect (it

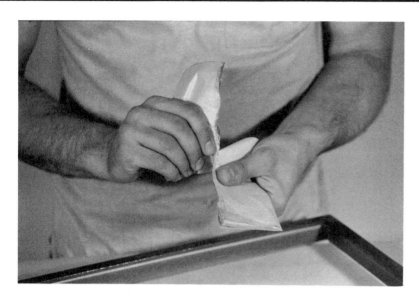

1 Tear the book of metal leaf in half parallel to the spine. For smaller work tear the book into even smaller pieces.

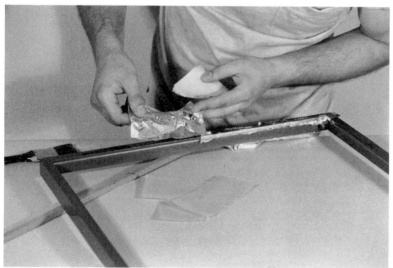

2 Lay each piece carefully in place overlapping about ¼" (.64 cm). As you apply, try not to wrinkle the leaf.

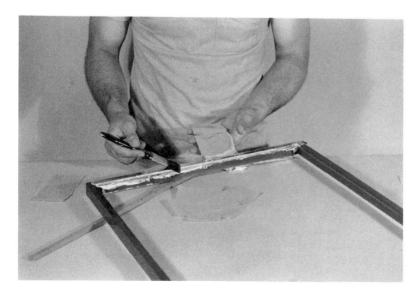

3 To make sure there is good contact all over, pat the leaf into place with a soft brush. Later you will need the same brush to remove the excess leaf.

works best with real gold). This technique requires you to brush against the laps of the leaf. Unlike brushing with the laps which conceals the joins, this backbrushing tends to show the edges, making it obvious that the frame has been leafed, not painted.

If you intend to show some of the red base underneath the leafing, do it before you polish the gold with cotton or velvet. This technique is best done with fine steel wool by passing the pad gently along the highest crest and highlights of any carved or molded areas. Be careful not to overdo this, however; the red base will show more after the shellac has been applied, which is the next step.

After you have wiped away all particles, apply one coat of white shellac. If you want a deeper gold look use half orange shellac. This seals the leaf and protects it from the toner. Shellac is the proper sealer because it is soluble only in alcohol, a solvent not used in the toning solution. The natural color of shellac is orange or amber. (It is made from the resinous secretions of the lac bug, a scaly insect native to Asia.) The white or clear form of shellac is bleached. The orange shellac is used as a kind of gold lacquer to turn the aluminum to gold when doing the silver-gilt finish. This method can produce a high-key gold, the depth of which is controlled by the color of the toning glaze. An example of the silver-gilt finish appears on the calligraphy framed with a silk mat and gold bevel (see page 00). Silver-gilt was chosen because real gold is in the calligraphy itself and also on the bevel; and in this context, the combination of tones works very well.

TONING

Toning is a procedure that is done to soften the garish look of metal leaf. The raw leaf, either the gold metal leaf or the aluminum, is so shiny and cheap looking that it really must be toned down to make it acceptable. Only real gold can show its bare face. Real silver (or palladium) can also be left without toning, but all others must be subdued in some way. The method I use most often is an oil glaze. The glaze or toning color may be either japan or oil. The japan will dry rapidly necessitating working quickly, so perhaps it is best to use oil color until you are really confident. The basic glaze color for most gold frames is burnt umber, tinted with a touch of black (to tone down the red). The basic toning color for aluminum is raw umber mixed with black. If you are going for silver-gilt, then use the same color as you would for gold. If you would like a deep-toned red tone, usually called Roman gold, you can use metal leaf and add a little burnt sienna to the usual glaze. Of course, these are not rules, just recipes that I have learned through practice. You may find that you prefer Mars brown or something else; it's even possible to use green or blue or whatever you like.

Begin the toning process by breaking up your chosen oil color with a little turpentine. Using a brush to stir the solution (a tool more efficient than a stick), add a few drops of boiled linseed oil and a little more turpentine. Then test the glaze on the back of the frame or on a scrap that has been prepared in the same way. Paint the toning solution on, making sure to get it into any deep recesses or grooves. Next, wipe the surface gently with cheesecloth or other soft material, such as an old T-shirt. The object of the wiping is to both distribute the color and to remove it at the same

time, leaving a partially even effect. It is this consistency of the glaze that makes the difference between success or failure. The glaze must be thin enough to flow when brushed and to leave a transparent film; but it must be thick enough to hold its place when wiped or stippled. Too much turpentine will cause the glaze to run and drip; too much oil will cause it to slide and be sticky. Too much pigment will cause it to be opaque and unglazelike.

After you have completed the first wiping, take a large, soft, fluffy brush—natural pig bristle is the best (Chinese if possible)—and stipple the surface with the dry brush, distributing the glaze into an even layer that doesn't show the brushwork. Then go back and gently wipe just the highlights with a soft cloth. Leave the full tone of the glaze in the deep recesses and use the stippling brush again if needed to get a fine gradation from highlight to shadow. This is quite easy to do; with a little practice you will be sailing through this stage.

This next step requires a little more skill and judgment. Fly-specking (which I define as an artful spattering) is what distinguishes a good glazing job. To do this, dip an old toothbrush into your toning color and then make a small puddle of it on the paper. Since some of the solvent has been absorbed into the paper, the color is now stronger. If it isn't, you can add a small amount of pigment to get a denser color. Then, using a small flat stick, strike the toothbrush repeatedly until the right-size specks are made on the test paper. To do this, you should push the bristles lightly over the edge of the stick. This technique fires the specks away from you and onto the frame. Be careful as you do this; too little is better than too much. If some spots are too large, blot them immediately with soft cloth. Do not wipe! Blotting blends with the finish, wiping destroys it. To help blend mistakes, a stippling brush can be used. This brush should be kept as clean as possible throughout this procedure by wiping it frequently on a clean rag. After the job is completed, wipe it immediately on a turpentine-coated rag and then wash it with soap and water.

In most cases, the toning process ends here. However, if heavier effects are desired, a coat of shellac and another glazing can be added using another color. Finally, it is sometimes desirable to dust with rottenstone after the glaze is dry, which will give a soft and dusty effect. This step should be done the day after the toning. Wipe the rottenstone off except for that which remains in deep grooves, and quickly and gently apply paste wax to the highlights. Let dry twenty minutes and buff lightly with a soft cloth.

There are times when a little color introduced into the gilt frame will enhance the picture. The color should be applied after you have done the cotton or velvet rub but before the shellac sealer. Gold and black are classic examples of this; red is used sometimes, and olive green can be very handsome as well. The colonial-shape molding lends itself to painting color in the "cove," or concave area of the mold. Japan color is good for this, mixed with turpentine and a little boiled oil or varnish. After the color has been applied, let it dry and then shellac the whole frame. This way the color will be sealed against the solvent in the toning. If you want a very subtle, soft effect, add burnt umber to black. Remember that any color is altered by the addition of a glazing layer, so keep the color lighter than you want the finished effect to be.

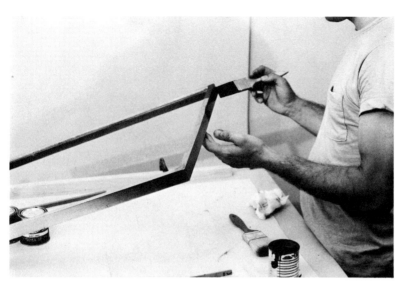

1 After all the leaf has been laid and shellacked, apply the toning color generously. The consistency is very important; it should be thin enough to flow when brushed, but thick enough to hold its place when wiped.

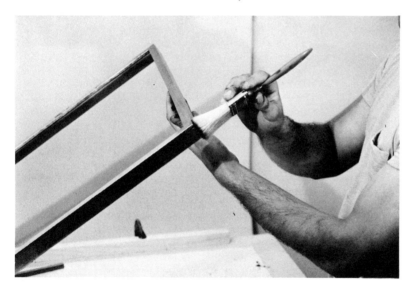

2 Wipe the toning color, leaving a kind of glazing on the gilded surface. Work on only one side of the frame at a time. Then stipple the just-wiped surface of the frame to distribute the glaze into an even tone. Use the tips of the bristles of a dry, fluffy brush.

3 After the stippling and second wiping of highlights or edges, apply the "fly-specks." Working from a puddle of toning glaze set nearby, spatter the frame by means of a toothbrush rubbed over the edge of a small flat stick. If too large a spot appears, blot it with a dry cloth but do not wipe—wiping will erase the specks.

GLASS CUTTING

Although many people think that glass cutting is a difficult task, it actually is not. And, if you don't have the inclination to cut glass on your own, you can always go to your local glazier and let him cut it for you. If that's your decision, be sure to take the frames with you so there is no mistake in the size you need. I do feel, however, that you can benefit by learning to cut your own glass, if only for the satisfaction of being able to do something most people think is difficult.

The tools required for glass cutting are very elemental and not very expensive. First, you'll need an inexpensive glass cutter. I suggest the Fletcher no. 2, the kind that has a ball at the end of the handle, and is used by many professional glaziers. You'll also need a straight-edge or T-square, some masking tape, a ruler, perhaps a pair of gas pliers; or, if you care to make the investment, glass pliers and a little kerosene are just about all that it takes to cut your own glass. The surface on which you cut need not be carpeted, although many glaziers work on a carpeted surface. My preference is to work on a smooth, flat table surfaced with Upson board. A really hard surface is not desirable, but a really soft one, such as a blanket, is not good either. The carpeted table at the glazier's allows the glass crumbs to fall into the pile, which makes it easier to continue working on the same surface. Eventually, however, the glazier must clean it or the buildup begins to cause scratches. On the Upson board surface, you can use a counter brush to sweep away the tiny chips that may scratch your glass.

Glass cutting is sort of a misnomer. You do not really "cut" glass—you score and break it. The Fletcher cutter I have recommended is the wheel type; there are others, but this type is universally used by most framers. An improvement on the Fletcher that you might consider is the longer-lasting tungsten carbide cutter. In the accompanying drawing, you will see the correct way of holding the glass cutter. You hold it between your first two fingers, not like a pencil. The forefinger puts pressure on the flattened top and the thumb helps to steady it in an upright position. The idea is that the wheel should be at as nearly a right angle to the glass as you are able to get it. While this position may seem awkward at first, it will become second nature to you in a short time. If you don't hold the cutter this way, eventually there will be undue wear on the wheel. There are situations where the cutter is run backward and pressure is applied by the thumb positioned on top, such as when you are cutting an oval shape, or when cuts are needed to follow curves and intricate shapes. This method is also used for cutting stained glass. But for our purposes, the cutter is held as shown, and the cut is made by drawing the cutter toward you. Allow one $\frac{1}{16}''$ (.16 cm) for the distance the wheel is from the side of the cutter and position your straight-edge. At this point, it may help to have pieces of masking tape on the glass in order to steady the straight-edge and to mark the place for the cut. A weight on the end of the straight-edge is also helpful. For this purpose, I use a terra-cotta tile or sometimes an iron. Or, you can have a friend firmly hold the end of the straight-edge down.

To make the score, take the cutter in hand, dip the wheel in kerosene, and roll it next to the straight-edge (pushing it away from you) to notch the edge of the glass. This creates the break point on the far edge. Now pull the cutter toward you with firm, even pressure. You will hear a kind of "burr" sound as the wheel scores the glass; as you become familiar with glass cutting, this sound will indicate to you whether you have made a good score or not.

After the glass has been scored, remove the straight-edge and immediately bring the waste area of glass off the edge of the table. Then, lift it in the air a few inches and with a brisk movement, bring it down sharply on the edge of the table. This action should cause the glass to divide along the score. However, if the score fails to divide the glass, don't restrike the score. Never go back over a score; it will either ruin your cutter or cause the glass to break in the wrong place. Instead, try tapping the glass from underneath along the score line. Pull the score over the edge of the table, and using the ball at the end of the cutter handle, strike gently and repeatedly under the glass until you see the fracture go through. Strike all along the length of the score but begin at the end or beginning. This method will usually cause the glass to divide. If it fails to do so, you may have to put this piece aside for some future use, such as a smaller picture. But don't get discouraged, soon you will be able to cut like a pro. If you are taking off just a small sliver, say a half inch or less, it's best to use pliers to make the break. First, do the scoring, then with the edge of the glass extended over the table, grasp the sliver with pliers near the end of the cut and apply pressure downward. Be sure to have the jaws of the pliers near but not over the score. With a little practice, the above information should be sufficient to give you control over the cutting of glass. Eventually, you will be able to cut the glass freehand on the frame itself.

Cutting odd shapes, such as an oval, will always be a bit of a challenge. To cut an oval, make a pattern of the shape and attach it to the underside of the glass. Make your score using the backhand hold of the cutter, pushing it away from you. Then make a number of cuts that project out in a radial manner from the edges of the score. Turn the whole piece over and tap gently from the back, using the ball of the cutter handle. This action should produce the break. If not, grozing may be necessary. Grozing is the term used to define the chewing away of sharp glass edges with pliers. Always cut the glass a little shy of the size of the frame. To remove a very small amount of glass is next to impossible. Never try to remove any piece less than $\frac{1}{4}''$ (.64 cm).

 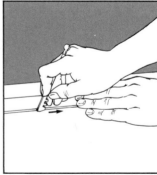

1 Place the straight-edge $\frac{1}{16}''$ (.16 cm) inside the desired measurement to compensate for the off-set of the steel wheel. (The end of it can be weighted or clamped to prevent slippage.) After dipping the cutter in kerosene, roll it forward to notch the far edge of the glass. Pull the cutter toward you with a steady, even pressure, and never go back over a score.

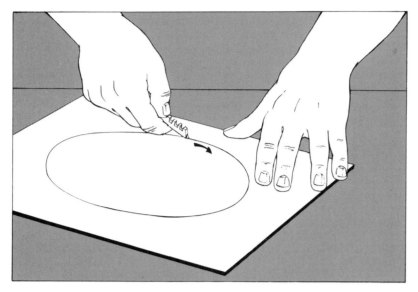

2 To cut an oval or circular shape, trace the rabbet from the frame or draw it with a compass or with string and push pins as illustrated in the section on oval matting (see page 38). Dip the cutter in kerosene and turning it upside down, start the score slightly off the line and let it move into the swing of the curve. Try to maintain a uniform pressure as you go forward. As you complete the score, bring the cutter back exactly to the point that it began the score and entered the cutting line.

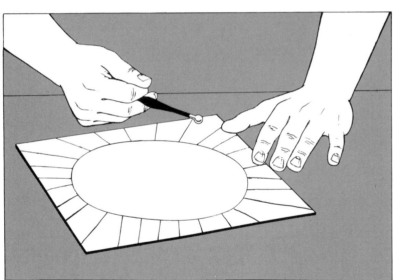

3 Make a number of radial scores out from the circle or oval to the edge of the glass. Don't begin these scores too close to the main score line. They can be made radially, as shown, or they can be made in a spinning or pinwheel fashion, radiating out from the main score tangentially.

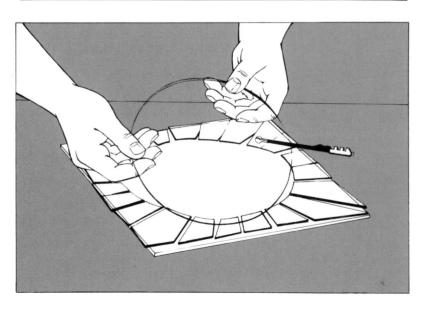

4 Remove the scored glass from the pattern and turn it face down. Using the ball end of the cutter, tap the back of the glass along the score line. Go all around the main score first then tap the radials. You will be able to see the score breaking through to the back of the glass.

FITTING OR ASSEMBLY

You are now ready for the stage known as fitting. In a commercial frame shop, the fitter is the person who does the fitting and makes the mats, while the frames are cut and joined together by someone called the joiner. There are often separate finishing people as well. Finally, the frame comes to the fitter and he assembles the work. He will have cut a piece of corrugated board or other stiffener to go behind the folder mat to form the actual backing. As mentioned before, if the picture is large enough, a strainer may also be needed for added support.

Prepare the table for the fitting process. I like to work on a surface covered by paper over a sheet of Upson board. This work surface is held in place by the "nailing edge," which is a length of hardwood clamped to the table edge. This piece of wood can be faced with leather or felt as are the vise jaws; but the plain wood will suffice. The purpose of the nailing edge is to hold in place the side of the frame as you are driving in the wire brads.

Before you begin the actual job of fitting, you'll need to wash the glass. First, place it flat on the table and rub vigorously with a damp cloth. Water is all you will need unless the glass is old and very dirty: glass from the glaziers is usually quite clean. Follow the damp washing with a dry cloth, rubbing the glass to a polish. Then pick the glass up carefully by its edges and turn it over. Clean the other side and position it over the matted work that is also positioned on its corrugated backing.

At this stage it's easier to get the entire sandwich of mat and glass into the frame by resting its side on the nailing edge. Then, lower the frame in place and check for any dirt that may have gotten between the glass and mat. If all is well, grasp the whole arrangement firmly and turn it over face down. With the frame held against the nailing edge, insert a ¾" (1.9 cm) no. 18 wire brad into the backing and flatten it against the board by pushing it down with your finger. Drive it half way into the molding. In larger frames you may find 1" (2.54 cm) brads preferable. This method of piercing the backing is known as "nailing on the mat" because the brad, when driven, should slide easily across the back of the mat. Be careful not to pierce the mat as you might strike the glass. If you find this nailing method too difficult, simply press the brad against the backing and nail it on the surface of the backing. There should be at least four brads per side with spaces of 4" to 5" (10 to 12.7 cm) between. Be sure to have brads approximately an inch from all corners. Of course, to nail it, you must turn the frame and place each side against the nailing edge. Lift the frame when turning rather than simply spinning it around on the paper; a leafed finish in particular can be abraded by this action. If you have difficulty moving the frame easily, try covering the surface with felt.

When you have completed the nailing, examine the assembly from the front to be sure that no dirt has crept in during the nailing process. If you see any dirt, you'll need to pull out the brads and carefully remove the offending matter. The best tool for the removal of brads is a pair of "diagonals," which are cutters used by electricians. Ordinary gas pliers will do, of course, but the diagonals will give you a better hold on the brad. Push the jaws into the backing and grasp the brad near the place where it enters the molding, then with a rocking motion grab the nail with the cutters against the edge of the molding. Because of the leverage gained, the brad will slide out easily, which is much better than trying to pull it out tug-of-war style.

The back should now be sealed against the entry of dust. A sheet of brown paper can be used for this purpose by gluing the paper to the back of the molding and trimming the excess with a razor blade. An easier approach is to use strips of gummed paper tape, a method which leaves the backing board exposed.

The screw eyes should be an appropriate size for the frame. Your judgment will tell you when the size is right. The number 212–1/2 is suitable for many frames; number 215–1/2 is good for smaller pieces. Very large frames with strainers should not be hung by screw eyes at all; they require heavy-duty mirror hangers. These are applied with two screws of appropriate size and are best used with a loop of wire on each hanger rather than one piece connecting the two. Hang from two nails a few inches inside the frame line. If one side seems to hang a little low, you can shorten it by simply giving the loop a twist or two. In any case a picture should always be hung from two nails. When a single wire crosses over two nails—placed 6" to 8" (15.2 to 20.3 cm) apart—it prevents the picture from seesawing out of level as well as keeps everything hanging straight. If you are using a lightweight picture wire (no. 1 or no. 2) and need to hang a heavier-weight picture, loosely twist two or three of the wires together for extra strength.

Frames requiring strainers usually have been dust-sealed before the strainer was inserted, which makes it easier later to change the picture or replace the glass. If the screws are placed from the outside of the frame to hold the strainer, they should be of a nonrusting variety, such as brass, a material which looks good with most hardwoods. If the frames have a silver look, it's best to use plated screws or stainless steel.

Sometimes in the fitting process you will need to take into account the space that exists between glass and mat. There are two ways to do this. One is to insert a spacer, which can be a small strip of wood (model maker's balsa is handy for this purpose). After the glass is cleaned and placed in the frame, wood strips are inserted to fit all around the edge. To hold the strips in place, use three or four little dots of glue on the edges that touch the back of the rabbet.

If you need greater space between glass and mat, you may need wider wood strips. For example, you may want to accommodate three-dimensional objects; in that case, because the strips will be visible, you'll need to paint or cover them with fabric. These strips normally don't protrude in front of the rabbet; they are usually no more than ³⁄₁₆" (.48 cm). The strips can be made of wood, double-thick matboard or chipboard, or Upson board.

The second method creates space by the use of a frame within a frame. The inner frame actually contains the backing and the object held in its rabbet; then the entire arrangement is placed in another frame deep enough to contain the inner frame. The glass is set between the two frames. This arrangement makes the frame more imposing and also adds more decorative possibilities.

Although the esthetics of picture hanging are somewhat arbitrary, a general rule is that the center of a picture should fall 62" (157.48 cm) from the floor. This so-called eye-level is a pleasing height for most things. Of course, sometimes you will want to hang one picture above another and do groupings; in that case, different levels will be called for.

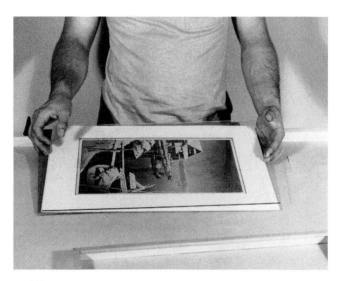

1 Wash glass thoroughly with a damp cloth. Then place the mat over the glass and check for any dirt that may have gotten between them.

2 With the frame braced against the nailing edge, pierce the backing board with a wire brad and flatten it with your index finger while you drive it into the molding. The tool shown here is an upholsterers' tack hammer.

3 After attaching screw eyes and wire, the sandwich of glass, art, mat, frame, and backing is complete.

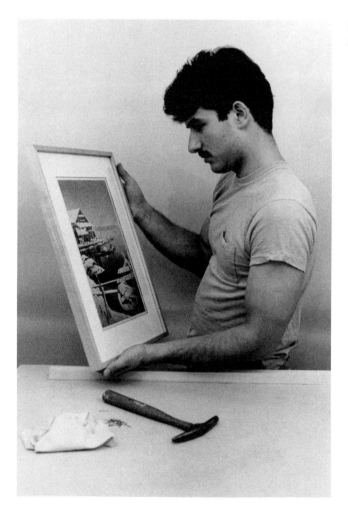

THE DRIFTWOOD FRAME

In this demonstration, the finish of the frame is more important than the matting. The piece shown here is a watercolor of the seashore. The nature of the subject matter makes this painting a perfect subject for the driftwood frame. Although the term implies fakery, in reality the "driftwood" of the framing trade is not very similar to real driftwood, just like "barn-siding" doesn't mean actual weathered wood. What is really meant by this term is a method of giving a soft and worn effect to new wood.

With minor variations, the techniques for accomplishing the driftwood look is uniform throughout the framing trade. The following is my method, and, in time, I hope you will develop and hand down your own. The driftwood method belongs to the category of distressed finishes, a system which consists of scratching, denting, scraping, or otherwise "wearing" the wood surface with various tools, then staining it dark. Most typical staining is done with an umber color (oil or japan) and turpentine. Sometimes a little black or a little red can also be added—the variations depend on individual choice.

After staining, a coat of shellac is added to seal the color. Then a gray wash of casein paint (white with a little black and a little umber, rather thinner than would ordinarily be used for painting) is applied and immediately wiped with a damp cloth. The wiping gives a somewhat transparent effect, just a film of gray over the surface. Practice will show you just how much wiping to do. If desired, you can also use alkyd paint, the difference being that you must wipe with a turpentine-soaked rag rather than water.

After the gray wash is dry, it needs to be "roughed up" with sandpaper or steel wool. Coarse sandpaper works best; it leaves little lines in the gray that show through the undercolor. You can heighten this effect by drybrushing in a number of colors (often taken from the colors in the painting) onto the surface just before the gray wash. Once again, you should seal off this layer with shellac before applying the wash. An alternative way of introducing various colors into a finish is to spatter them onto the gray wash after it has been completed; use steel wool or sand, and then spatter the colors.

A casein wash changes tone rather radically after it has dried. If you find it too light, you can make it darker with a wash of dirty turpentine. Apply this solution liberally and rub briskly with a dry cloth to dry—then sand or use steel wool.

The last stage of this type of finish is typically "flyspeck-ing," or flecking with dots of color, from a toothbrush rubbed over a stick or thumb. When dry, this spattering can be followed by a light waxing with paste wax on the high points. A rottenstone dusting may be added to this finish, but often when casein is used, it is not, because casein itself is dry and dusty. If you use alkyd oil paint for the wash, then you could use rottenstone to dull the toning. Stop when you believe that a satisfactory look for the piece has been achieved.

As you will see in the demonstration that follows, the driftwood effect was done for the outside molding only; the liner is painted a soft off-white.

1 Measure for the mat with a folding rule and add the mat width to the size of the opening. This gives you the size of the mat, backing boards, frame, and glass.

2 After cutting the mat and backing to size, lay out the opening on the back of the mat pieces. Use the marking block and folding rule to mark three dots.

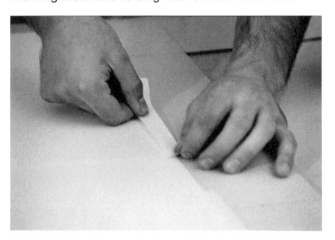

3 Use the Dexter cutter to cut the opening. Insert the cutter blade into the line just outside the corner and place the straight-edge up against the body of the cutter and parallel to the line a little more than ¼″.

4 Join the undermat to the backing with hinges made of linen tape.

5 Position the watercolor in the opening with the mat closed. Use a folding rule as a weight to keep it from moving. Then, open the mat and make the attachment by forming two linen tape hinges at the top corners. In this case, there was room to do this on the front of the paper because the mat overlaps some of the edge.

6 Cut the frame liner from ½″ (1.27 cm) box molding, using the miter saw and steel miter box. Then, using the liner to mark the size of the outer frame, cut that out also. This molding is a 2″ (5.08 cm) wide double bevel produced on the table saw.

7 Join the outer frame using corner clamps, nails, and glue. This method lets you get it done without a vice.

8 Take white casein paint and apply it to the face and lip of the liner. It won't be necessary to paint the side or back because the liner can't be seen.

9 Next, to achieve the distressed driftwood effect, employ various tools to scratch, puncture, dent, or wear the surface of the frame.

10 Apply a coat of dark stain. In this example, burnt umber with turpentine is used. You can also use oil or japan color, or you might choose a commercial stain. In any case, after this coat has dried, seal it with shellac. Don't forget to thin the shellac slightly with alcohol.

11 Now apply a coat of warm gray casein paint thinned with water to the consistency of milk or light cream. The gray is made by mixing a little burnt umber and a little black casein colors into white.

12 Wipe the gray wash with a damp cloth. This will thin the gray on the surface to an almost transparent water glaze. The color should remain gray, however. The full strength can be seen in the scratches. Wipe one side of the frame at a time, because the casein dries too rapidly to do the entire frame. Turn the frame each time so that the side you are wiping is in the same position and receives the same lighting conditions. This will help you achieve a uniform effect.

13 After the casein has dried, use coarse steel wool or sandpaper to scratch the gray coating in order to show dark stain beneath.

14 Use a toothbrush rubbed over a stick to splatter light gray, blue-gray, brown, and almost black speckles onto the molding. You can use oil or japan color and turpentine for the pigment. Blot the color off with a rag and scratch through large splotches with sandpaper.

15 Cut and wash the glass, then place it over the picture and corrugated backing. Rest the stack on the nailing so that you can lower the liner onto it. Turn the whole package face down, and with it against the nailing edge, nail the picture into the liner.

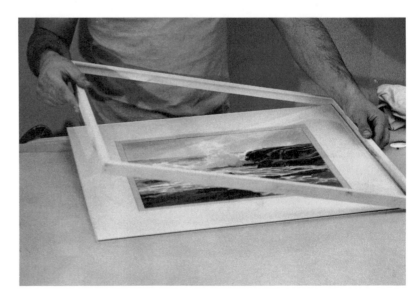

16 Place the liner in the outer frame and nail it diagonally through the liner into the outer frame.

17 Apply glue all around the back of the frame and cover with a sheet of brown paper to act as a dust seal. (This is an alternate method to sealing with gummed paper tape.) Cut excess paper with a razor blade using the middle finger as a guide to make the cut clean at the edge.

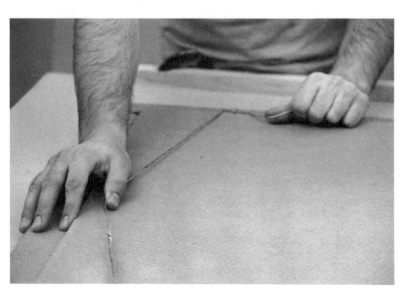

18 Attach screw eyes and wire. Test to make sure the length is correct before attaching the wire to the second screw eye.

THE "J" FRAME

This delicate pencil drawing of a monkey reaching for an apple was done on rather lightweight paper. The work of Reuben Kadish, it dates from the 1930s. It was originally framed by a commercial framer who apparently was unaware of the dangers of rubber cement. When the artist noticed it turning brown, he removed the drawing from the mounting board, but the damage had already been done. Although badly discolored, the drawing is still very beautiful, so my first consideration was to try to frame it in a way that plays down its deteriorated condition. To accomplish this, I treated the discoloration as part of the piece itself, using a tan mat (Bainbridge 412) to harmonize with the drawing rather than set it apart with white, which would have only emphasized the yellowed paper.

The choice of possible frames for this drawing was, of course, large. A section frame in black or gold was a possibility, but not silver, as silver wouldn't have provided enough "weight" for the drawing because although the lines are delicate the forms are quite massive. My next choice was a wooden box-style frame painted charcoal to reflect the graphite line, but the squareness of the box-style edge left me desiring more complexity. So I decided on the rounded face of the "J" molding, and kept the idea of painting the frame charcoal to pick up the graphite in the drawing. Then I reconsidered again—the charcoal seemed too cold and abstract for such a natural subject. At that point, it occurred to me that I should complement the drawing with a natural material. Because the color relates to the piece itself, I chose cherry wood to fashion the frame.

To make the "J" molding, I cut strips of cherry wood on the table saw pushing it through the ⅜″ (.95 cm) round-over router bit to create its rounded face. Then I went back to the saw to make the rabbet.

After cutting, the molding must be joined. Here, I used the glue-and-nail method shown in the cutting and joining part of the framing section (see page 78). After the glue had set, I filled the corners and the nail holes with a wood putty of a similar color to the cherry. It's called "red birch" and is also good for red oak. All three of these woods are close in color and value. If the putty color is not sufficiently close, however, you will be forced to match it yourself with the use of japan colors or oils. Many times I have stuffed holes and flaws with putty that doesn't match and simply painted it to match after I have applied the first coat of finish. The first coat of finish (shellac, varnish, lacquer, or Danish oil) turns the wood surrounding the puttied area to the finished color.

Once the final color of the wood has been established by the finish coat, apply color to the puttied area. Japan color is the easiest. There are ten basic colors that will enable you to match almost any wood color: striping white, burnt umber, raw umber, yellow ochre, raw sienna, burnt sienna, chrome green, ultramarine, chrome yellow, and black.

After the retouching has dried (if that step was necessary), apply a thinned-down coating of shellac. The usual proportion of alcohol should be one-third to two-thirds shellac. If your shellac is a three-pound cut, then it needs no thinning. This coating should be allowed to dry at least two hours. It can then be sanded down with steel wool to produce a smooth, grain-filled surface to which you apply a natural wax finish of Butcher's wax. It enhances the natural color and grain of the wood and is quite simple to do. If you desire a slight sheen, buff the wood lightly with a soft cloth.

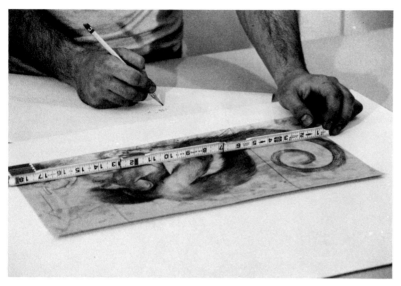

1 Using the folding rule to determine the size of the opening of the mat, allow about ⅜″ (.95 cm) all around the drawing to let it "float" on a piece of museum board (ivory). Then measure 3″ (7.62 cm) for the top and sides and 3¼″ (8.57 cm) for the bottom. The opening should measure 9¼″ × 18¾″ (23.5 × 47.6 cm). To arrive at the overall mat size, add the mat widths to the opening size, which gives you 15½″ × 24¾″ (39.37 × 62.87 cm). Cut two pieces of board to this size.

2 Using the Dexter cutter and the straight-edge, cut out the opening. The blade should be adjusted so that the tip pierces but does not penetrate the scrap board underneath. Position the straight-edge by piercing the board with the blade a little before the corner, then move the straight-edge against the body of the cutter, making it parallel to the line. Resting your hand on the cutter, push it forward to just beyond the far corner. Then lift the cutter, turn the mat, and insert the blade in the line of the adjacent side and repeat.

3 After you have cut the mat, lay it face down alongside the piece of museum board and join the two with hinges of linen tape. Next, position the drawing in the opening; it helps to place a small weight such as a book or the folding rule on the drawing to keep it from slipping.

4 Place a piece of tape on the museum board behind the upper corner of the drawing. This is done by forming a small loop around your fingertip with the adhesive side out, then flattening it onto the board or the back of the drawing. Note that it is placed in a vertical position so that it will be more resistant to rolling.

5 Turn your attention to the frame and cut the strips of molding using a steel miter box and a miter box backsaw. This cherry wood "J" molding was made on the router because standard moldings are not available in exotic woods such as cherry.

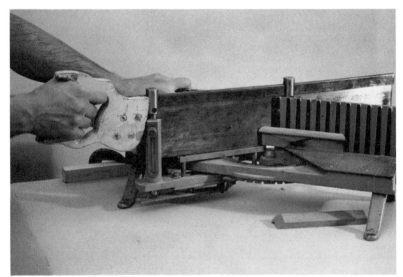

6 Join the cut lengths of cherry in the vice using glue and nails. Because cherry is a hardwood, it is necessary to predrill guide holes for the nails. With the corner still held in the vise, use a nail set to punch the head of the nail just under the surface of the molding.

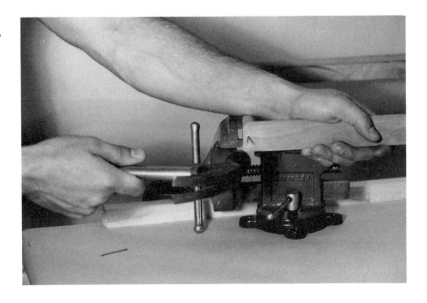

7 Apply a premixed wood putty of similar color to the wood and press it into the nail holes.

8 Sand the wood putty and touch up the surface of the frame. The corners should be lightly rounded to eliminate sharpness.

9 Apply shellac to the frame. To promote drying and allow for greater penetration, cut the shellac with about one-third alcohol. After the shellac has dried, use steel wool to remove it from the surface while leaving the grain filled. Fine steel wool will leave the surface very smooth. When done, wipe to remove dust.

10 Apply a good quality paste wax. Allow it to dry half an hour, then buff to a low sheen with a soft cloth and the finish is complete. This is called a wax finish and is very simple to do.

11 It is now time to cut the glass. Note how the cutter is held and remember to dip it in kerosene before using. Mark your measurements with small pieces of tape on the surface of the glass, then rest the ruler or straight-edge on them; they will help to prevent slipping as well as give you a mark. The measurement should be made 1/16″ (.16 cm) shy of the cut.

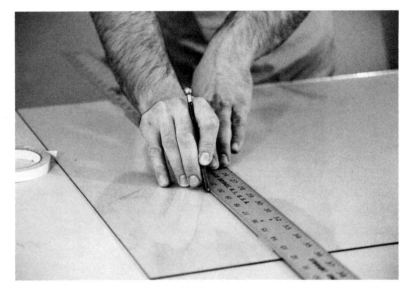

12 After washing the glass, place it over the mat and drawing, which has had a backing of corrugated board added. Rest the stack on the nailing edge and inspect for dirt. Then with the stack resting on the nailing edge, insert the entire sandwich into the frame. Never try to place the work in the frame by dropping it in with the frame lying face down. If you do, there will most certainly be dirt in under the glass when you turn the picture face up.

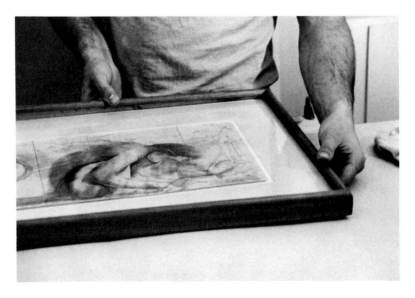

13 With the frame face down and resting against the nailing edge, drive in no. 18 wire brads to hold the work against the glass. Pierce the corrugated backing about ½″ (1.27 cm) in from the frame. Then press the brad down flat with the tip of your finger and drive it into the molding with the tack hammer. This procedure is called "nailing on the mat," because the nail is sliding across the back of the folder mat as it is buried in the backing. Apply the nails 4″ or 5″ (10.16 or 12.7 cm), making sure that some are near the corners.

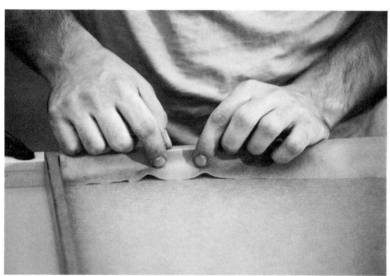

14 Use gummed brown paper tape to make a dust seal and conceal the edge of the backing and the nails. Cut the tape to fit, wet with water, and apply neatly.

15 Place the screw eyes in the upper third of the frame, so that the frame can hang flat on the wall. The awl shown here is a useful tool for inserting the screw eyes. It is used to punch holes for starting and then to turn with leverage. Cutters or pliers can also be helpful. Attach picture wire to the screw eyes and the job is complete.

THE SHADOW-BOX FRAME

To demonstrate the use of a shadow-box frame, I chose a flattened beer can found in the street to be the subject. Another can (soy sauce) shows an alternate type of shadow box. Both of these cans are brightly colored, so a playful treatment will emphasize that aspect. The beer can is mounted on white linen-covered board. The separation strips, which are 1″ (2.54 cm) deep, are painted bright red, and the frame is a box style finished with aluminum leaf.

The soy sauce can is mounted on plush red velvet. The inner frame, which serves as the separator, is leafed with gold metal leaf and is not toned. The outer frame is a satin black O'Keeffe molding. The size of the frame is important here. Enough space should be given to allow breathing room for the object, but it is also good to retain a sense of preciousness by keeping the frame small.

Because the cans have no real value, they were simply glued with epoxy to the back. If you are framing more valuable three-dimensional objects, you might prefer to "sew" them on with thread or wire. Objects such as fans, jewelry, or lace would be damaged by glue. Dried flowers

were at one time a favorite shadow-box item; and many bridal bouquets have been preserved in this way. A christening dress, a pair of ladies' kid gloves from Civil War days, a number of military medals, a small doll with china head, a grandmother's rosary, and a very old pocketwatch are among the many items I have framed for various people.

Should you find a need for especially deep moldings and you are not able to find them, I suggest that you make your own shadow box from plain strips of wood and then, to create a rabbet, face it with an unrabbeted strip of molding. Make sure that it is wider than the thickness of the strips used to make the box. Upson board is very useful for making the separation strips and the backing boards. You can cut it to any width or size you wish with a utility knife and a straight-edge. You will need to make repeated passes with the knife, so do not attempt to cut through with one pass. In calculating the depth of your separation strips, try to leave enough space in the back to allow at least ¼″ (.64 cm) behind the back board for the screw eyes and wire. This allows the box to hang flat on the wall.

1 Use the utility knife to cut a piece of Upson board to fit the frame. Determine the size by visually trying the can on smaller and larger pieces of scrap board until you achieve the right proportion.

2 Apply glue with a brush to the board, brushing it out well so that puddles of glue don't come through the fabric. The fabric used here is white linen.

3 Smooth the fabric onto the glued surface and trim the edges with scissors or a razor blade.

4 Position the can and glue it to the board with epoxy.

5 Cut a 2″ (5.08 cm) box molding upside down, using the steel miter box and miter saw. (Some moldings are held more easily upside down.)

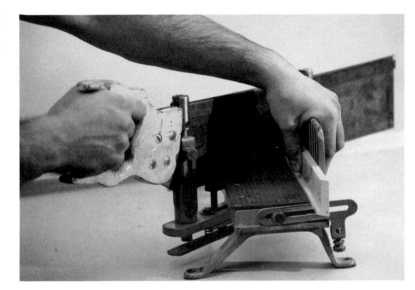

6 After the frame has been cut and joined, sand it down to make it smooth.

7 Apply a coat of red casein to the frame to act as a filler and to resemble a red clay base of water gilding. When the casein has dried, sand the wood with fine sandpaper; then recoat with the casein, sand again, and shellac twice to produce a good foundation for the size.

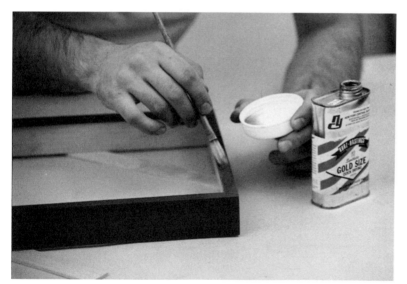

8 Coat the frame with gold size and allow to dry for over an hour. Then test the size for its readiness to receive the leaf.

9 When the tact is just right, lay the leaf from the book and pat in place with a clean, dry, soft brush.

10 Next, cut the glass to its appropriate size. Remember to pay attention to how the cutter is held. Dip the cutter in kerosene. Begin the cut by notching the far edge, first rolling the cutter forward then drawing it toward you. As you guide the cutter along the straight-edge, keep a firm, even pressure.

11 Immediately after scoring, snap the glass. This snap was made by placing the ball of the cutter exactly under the score and pressing down on both sides at the same time. Another method is to bring the score to the edge of the table, raise the extended part of the glass a few inches, and bring the score down sharply on the edge of the table.

12 Wash the glass thoroughly on both sides and place it carefully in the frame.

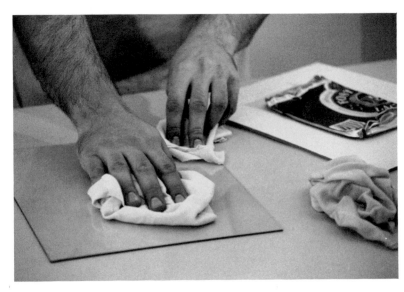

13 Apply dots of glue to the backs of the separation strips and put them in place against the glass. This creates a second rabbet where the backing board will sit.

14 Nail in the board that has the can attached. Seal the edges with tape for a dust seal.

15 Attach screw eyes and wire. Make sure that the size of the screw eyes are appropriate for the size of the frame. If you are using lightweight picture wire, and the framing sandwich is too heavy, loosely twist two or three of the wires together for extra strength.

THE SHADOW-BOX FRAME

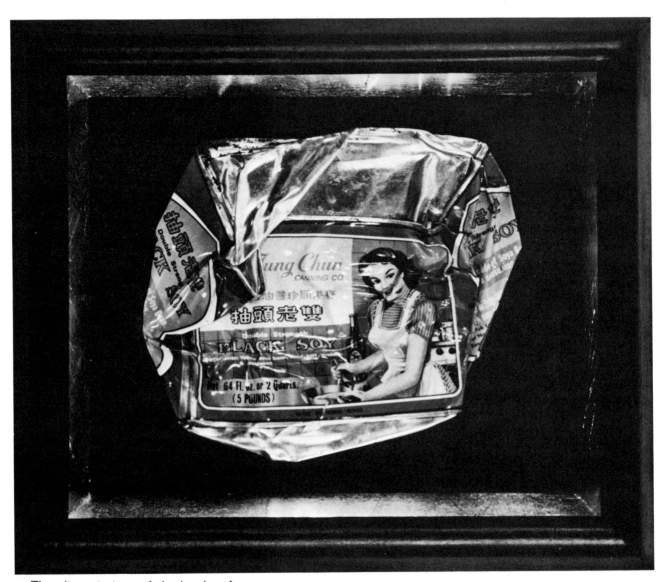

The alternate type of shadow-box frame.

THE SILVER SECTION FRAME

Of all types of metal frames on the market today—and there are many—the most popular by far is the silver section frame. This is true because it is a relatively simple and available framing solution; it is probably sold in every art supply store in the country. The silver section frame makes a handsome frame for most photographs and for many works of graphic art. And because of its standardization and highly reusable quality, it is also a practical solution as an exhibition frame. But for all its assets, I fear that the silver section has become the framing crutch of our time; and I, for one, do not advise its use for all purposes. The imposition of this ubiquitous frame has given a characterless quality to the art of framing, depriving it of its essential function, which is to accent and emphasize the inherent qualities of the piece being framed.

The silver section frame is made by a number of manufacturers. The products vary slightly in width of molding or in finish of sides (some have brushed effects, others are shiny), or in the manner of joining the corners or

hangers. They are all essentially aluminum extrusions with three grooves along the inside of the sections. The first and largest of these grooves lies behind the face; it creates the rabbet space into which the sandwich of glass, mat, art, and backing is inserted. This area also contains a small slot into which one piece of the corner-joining hardware slides. One or two more grooves occur at the back of the extrusion, into which the corner joining device is inserted along with a hanger on two sides. These joining devices generally consist of right-angle metal pieces about ⅜" (.95 cm) wide, which are thick enough to almost fill the groove. They are held in place when pushed together by tightening a set screw that keeps the angle from sliding out of the groove. Some of these set screws require special hex wrenches to tighten (they are provided in the kit), but some are tightened with ordinary slotted or Phillips-type screwdrivers. The frames are sold in two pieces to the package; so, to make a frame, you must buy one package of each dimension.

THE SILVER SECTION FRAME

1 In this example, an 8″ × 10″ (20.32 × 25.4 cm) color photograph is framed by a standard size 16″ × 20″ (40.64 × 50.8 cm) silver section. First, measure the size of the opening needed. Subtract this from the size of the frame and divide the left over space to make even borders on the sides. Determine also the size of the area that goes above and below the photograph. In general, the narrower border looks better on top.

2 Lay out the mat on the back and cut the bevels with the Dexter cutter. Insert the blade of the cutter into the line a little beyond the corner. Then align the straight-edge against the body of the cutter and parallel to the line. The cutter should be a little more than ¼″ (.64 cm) from the line. Place a weight on the far end of the straight-edge or clamp it. Then push the cutter away from you guiding along the straight-edge until you have slightly passed the far corner. Turn the mat to an adjacent side and repeat.

3 Fasten the mat to the backing with tape. The one shown here is Filmoplast-P, but linen tape works well, too.

4 Position the photograph in the opening, holding it in place with the ruler or other weight. Then place two tape hinges on the top edge.

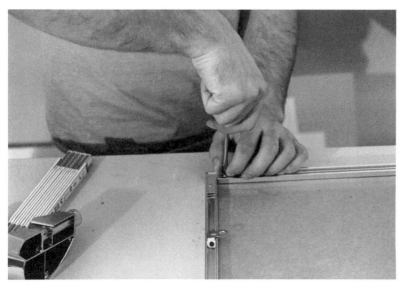

5 Put a piece of corrugated backing behind the mat and a clean piece of glass in front. Slide the sandwich into the assembled three sides of the frame. Add the fourth side (in this case, the top side) and screw the corners together.

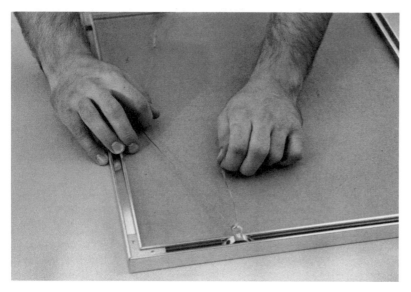

6 Add the wire to the hanger rings, which had been inserted before the top edge of the frame was screwed.

THE BLACK SECTION FRAME

The section frame is ordinarily associated with the polished or satin-finish look of aluminum, but it also comes in gold anodized and a variety of colors, the most useful of which is black. Many framed pieces look best in black. The black section frame, because it is metal, presents a smaller face than a wood frame. This delicate line of black is just the right accent for such things as documents, posters, and many photographs. The calligraphy piece shown here was done to identify the subjects of the paintings on the Sistine Chapel ceiling. It was framed first with the edges of the piece close to the black frame. Then, to set the piece off a bit more, I spray-mounted it on charcoal-colored matboard.

Instructions for assembling these frames are included in the section frame package, and close attention to them will yield good results. However, you should be aware of potential problems. For example, if you find the section corners won't close completely, check to see that you haven't put the corner angle in backward. Many brands have a slight bend in the angle that will force the corner to close. Also, when using glass, it's not a good idea to go larger than 24″ × 30″ (60.9 × 76.2 cm) because the weight will cause the corners to open eventually.

One method you can use to make a larger frame in this style is to use the section pieces made for framing canvas on stretchers. With these, you can place your glass, mat, and backing, then measure the remaining space in the back of the frame and fill it with a lap-jointed frame of wood known as a strainer, or retainer. The retainer serves the same function as the stretcher on a canvas: the weight of the contents is borne by it, and the frame becomes merely a decorative edging. With this system you can go quite large: perhaps up to 40″ × 60″ (101.6 × 152.4 cm) (standard oversize matboard), or even as much as 48″ × 72″ (121.9 × 182.8 cm). After this point the glass becomes a problem because you must move to ³⁄₁₆″ (.48 cm), which is very heavy. As an extra safety precaution for larger sizes, you should drill the frame pieces from the side and place screws into the strainer. Larger pieces should not be hung from a wire stretched across the back; they should be attached to the strainer by individual loops on each side with a heavy-duty bail-style mirror hanger.

1 Using the hardware and directions for the brand frame you have purchased, screw the pieces of the black metal section together at the corners.

2 Place the bottom piece, or final section, in position and tighten it securely with screws.

THE EASEL-BACK

There are many ways of making easel-backs for picture frames. In commercial frames for photographs, you often see this type of back made of cardboard or wire. I have a favorite easel-back that I make. The easel-back is made of double-thick matboard and is covered with a plush red velvet. The tie between the backing and the "leg," or hinged part, is maroon grosgrain ribbon, and the lining of the leg is marblelized endpaper. The square tab at the top of the leg is attached to the backing with linen tape hinges, glue, and four brass paper-fasteners. The back is attached to the frame by nailing with brass escutcheon pins (domed-headed brass nails) at neat intervals all around the edge.

Before you make the easel-back part of the frame, it's best to complete the frame itself; at least, you should have the frame already cut and joined so that you are certain of the size, because the size of the easel-back depends on the width of the molding, not the size of the mat. Then cut a piece of double-thick matboard to the size of the outside of the frame, but make it a little shy to account for the thickness of the fabric cover, say 1/16″ (.16 cm). Cut another piece 1″ to 1½″ (2.54 to 3.8 cm) shorter than the height and 5″ (12.7 cm) wide. At 3″ (7.6 cm) from the end of this piece, draw a line. Set your straight-edge back about ¼″ (.64 cm) and cut a beveled edge toward this line. Now turn the longer piece around and cut the bevel toward the line on that end. To relieve any tendency to bind, these beveled edges should face each other at the point where the leg is hinged. These will be the only beveled cuts. Now mark the small piece and cut it 3″ (7.6 cm) square. Mark the beveled end of the long side 1″ (2.54 cm) in from each side, which will leave 3″ (7.6 cm), and cut it to a diagonal to the bottom corner to create the tapered leg. Keep in mind that the beveled edges go on the outside of the leg, that is, the side that will be covered with velvet.

To insert the grosgrain ribbon from the inside to the outside, make a slit with the mat knife about 2″ (5.08 cm) up from the bottom end. Glue the end of the ribbon to the surface for about an inch and cover this with a square of gummed paper tape. You will be doing this again with the other end inside the back. Now cover the boards with whatever fabric you have selected. This process is the same as for covered mats.

For velvet fabrics, paint the glue onto the board and lay it on the back of the fabric or lower the fabric into place as shown. With it in place, smooth all the nap in its natural direction. This step can be done by passing your fingers over the fabric or by using a soft hairbrush or clothing brush. Let the glue dry at least a half hour before continuing. During this interval you can cover the leg pieces; then trim all your edges with scissors and clip the corners at 45°. Be careful not to trim the corners too close or your board will show. Glue these sides down. Here we are using Poly-fab, but, as mentioned before, many other white glues will do. If you are covering your easel-back with a lighter fabric, such as a cotton broadcloth or some thin printed material of indeterminate origin, you might want to use the method discussed in covered mats. This method requires coating the surface and letting it dry, then attaching the fabric with a warm iron that reactivates the glue.

When the covering is finished, I like to place a strip of gummed paper tape around to seal the edges of the velvet and make it look neat. Of course, no one can see this when the frame is put together, but it helps to stop the shedding of the velvet and it just looks better if someone opens up the frame.

To connect the ribbon to the back, cut a slot and pass the end of the ribbon from the leg through the back at a point the same distance up from the bottom of the back. Make four small slots in the four corners of the 3″ (7.62 cm) square, and, observing which side has the bevel, lay it next to the leg piece. Join the square and the leg pieces with linen tape to create a hinge or use a piece of linen or other strong fabric and glue. Then, cut out a piece of lining paper and cut a slot for the ribbon. Slip the ribbon through and position the paper over the leg. Lift up one end of the paper and apply paste to the leg. Press the paper in place, then lift up the other end of the paper and glue it down.

Now the leg is ready to attach to the back, but it's best to wait an hour until all the glue has set. Then, using four paper fasteners and some glue on the back of the square piece, pierce the backing at four points and attach the leg. Turn the entire easel over and hammer the ends of the fasteners down and cover them with gummed paper tape.

The easel-back is now ready to attach to the frame. To do this, I use escutcheon pins, but there are other ways. Small brass oval-head screws with finishing washers are nice if you can find them. Double-stick tape is another possibility.

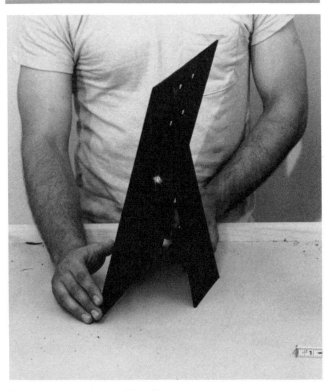

The completed easel-back.

1 Apply an even coat of paste to the backboard. Use watered-down bookbinders' P.V.A. or a similar glue.

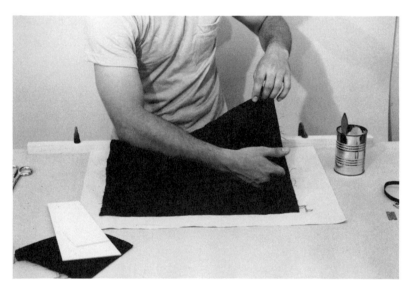

2 Carefully lay the velvet in place, smoothing it out and making sure not to get glue on the face. Never try to lift the velvet once you have smoothed it down.

3 Trim all sides to about 1" (2.54 cm) from the edge, then cut the corners off at 45°. Do not cut too close to the board at the corners.

4 After gluing down the flaps on the back, cover the ragged edges of the velvet with gummed paper tape to prevent fraying.

5 Make a slot with a knife and insert one end of a piece of grosgrain ribbon in the leg piece; glue it down for about 1″ (2.54 cm) and cover the end with a square of gummed paper tape. Proceed to cover the leg with velvet, using the same procedure as for the back.

6 Fold the flaps over and glue them down. To temporarily hold flaps down, use pieces of masking tape until you are ready to glue them.

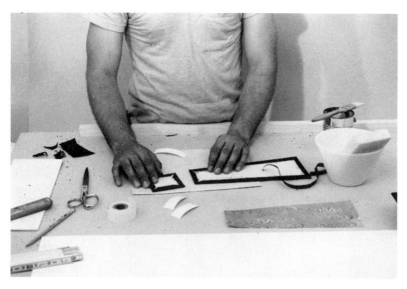

7 Join the leg piece to the small square at the point where their beveled edges face each other.

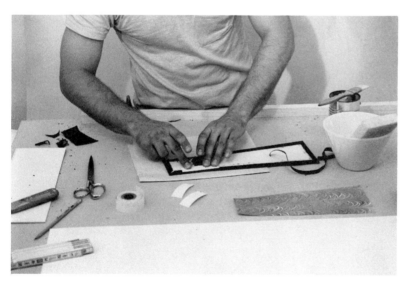

8 Apply linen tape to act as a hinge or use a piece of fabric with glue.

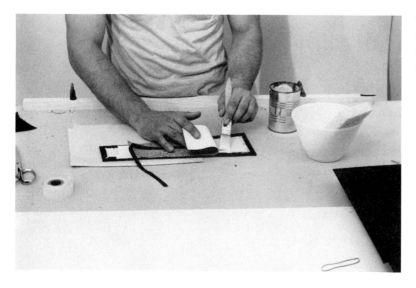

9 Cover the ragged edges and inside surface of the leg with a piece of decorative paper; in this case, it is marbelized end paper.

10 Glue one end of the leg from the ribbon down; then lift the other side of the paper, from the ribbon up, and glue that down.

11 Make a slot in the backing board at the same level as the slot in the leg and pass the end of the ribbon through. Determine the correct length to give a nice incline, then clip and glue the end.

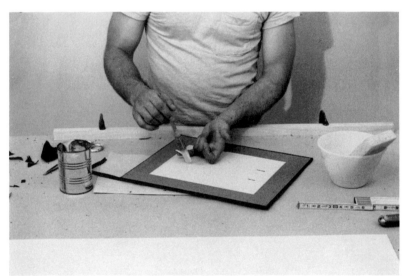

12 Cover the ribbon end with a square of gummed paper tape.

THE PLATFORM-STYLE FRAME

This stone lithograph by Mexican muralist David Siqueiros, is from that lively period of public art which existed in the 1930s. Because of this particular piece's history, I thought a platform-style frame of the type popular at the time would be most suitable. This frame consists of a dark (satin black) O'Keeffe used as a top molding, and is mounted on a 4″ (10.16 cm) oak platform stained a medium dark brown. There is no mat, but the print is dropped-on to a cream-colored museum board. It is kept from touching the glass by the insertion of ³⁄₁₆″ (.48 cm) separation sticks. This assemblage has a massive effect and requires a strong image, such as this larger than life-size head. Had I chosen to frame this piece in a more conventional manner, I would have used an ivory mat with a black bevel or a black undermat. A medium-heavy box or J-frame style would look good, too, preferably in walnut with a natural finish. It could also be done with a charcoal mat and an ivory frame. This piece would not look good in a gold or silver frame and certainly not in one that was thin. A linen-covered mat or any other textured effect wouldn't work well either. The lithograph has tone and texture of its own, which requires a stark treatment in the framing: simple matting, plain frame, and no carving or molding shapes with ornamental turns.

THE PLATFORM-STYLE FRAME

1 Measure the lithograph to determine the size of the frame. Since there is no mat to make for this piece, place the lithograph on a piece of museum board, leaving about ¾″ (1.91 cm) all around so that about ½″ (1.27 cm) will show when it is in the frame.

2 Attach the lithograph to the museum board with a roll of tape at the top corners. The tape roll or hinges used should be a neutral pH.

3 The base of the frame is made of oak plank mitered and joined in the usual way, but it should be reinforced by the addition of plywood corners glued and nailed to the back. This will prevent future separation of the molding caused by wood shrinkage.

4 Stain the platform frame with a mixture of umber and turpentine.

5 Wipe the stain to achieve a uniform effect and to reveal the grain.

6 Next, apply the shellac, which has been diluted slightly with alcohol. After the shellac has dried, rub the surface with steel wool, and then apply wax.

7 With the top molding lying face down, apply glue to the back.

8 Place the oak platform frame on the back of the top molding, nailing it to the top molding. Because it is oak, it is necessary to drill guide holes for the nails.

9 Cut and wash the glass. Then, nail the lithograph into the frame and make a dust seal with brown paper tape. Add screw eyes and hanging wire as the final step.

THE DOUBLE-SIDED FRAME

Occasionally the need arises to see both sides of a piece of art work because each side is of equal interest. In many cases, however, one side is more dominant and considered the "front," and the lesser side becomes the "back."

A vital characteristic common to double-sided frames is that they are invariably small, because it isn't practical to make a large frame that is meant to be handled. Some double-sided frames are made with bases so that they can stand by themselves. In the demonstration that follows, the piece was conceived as lying on a table in the manner of a book, so the frame was made to hold a page from a book— in this case, a very old book, a Bible printed in 1709.

I thought a rather heavy wooden frame would be appropriate for this purpose. Since double-faced moldings are not commercially available, I needed to make the molding with the aid of a table saw. If you want both sides of the frame to appear the same (as I did here), you need to cut away part of the depth of the frame from the back of a regular molding, then make two frames of equal size and attach them back to back. This effect is enhanced by placing yet another "frame" around the two frames; this creates another element in the design. One of the frames gets permanently glued into this "box," while the other is pinned with four escutcheon pins or four small screws.

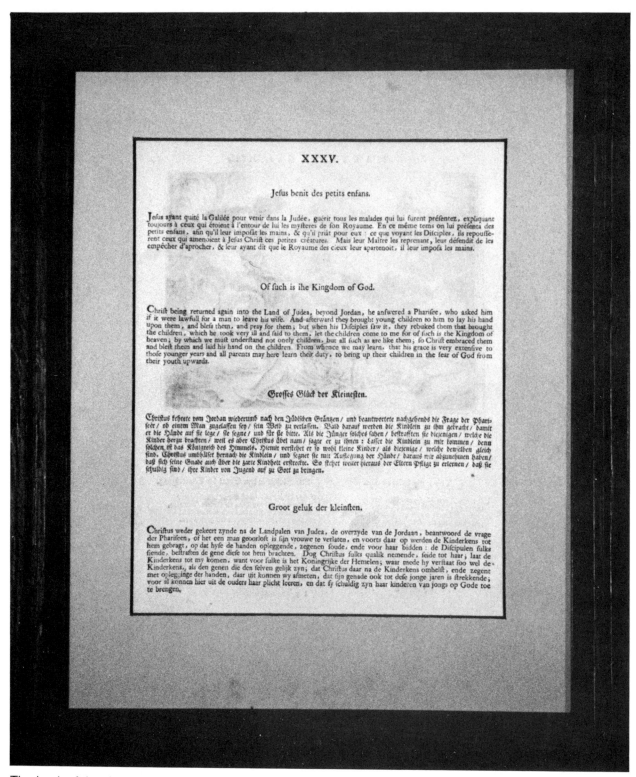

The back of the double-sided frame.

1 Cut two identical mats from tan (Bainbridge 412) matboard and color their bevels with black drawing ink. Attach the page to the "front" mat with framers' self-adhesive tape. If, as in this case, the paper is old and badly rippled, you can smooth it down by wetting it and taping the edges down to a board with gummed paper tape, a method similar to the manner of stretching watercolor paper. The paper would then have the chance to dry and pull taut as it shrinks.

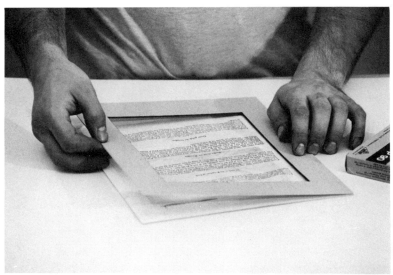

2 Place the second mat on the "back." Hold both mats in place by four rolls or rings of framers' tape made with the adhesive side out. You could also do this with a few spots of glue.

3 After the two pieces of glass have been cleaned, slip the entire sandwich into the groove of the assembled three sides of the frame, then cap the frame with the top side of the frame. Because both sides of the frame must be identical, the double-sided frame has a groove that is cut to the correct width rather than a conventional rabbet. The final step is to attach the top (fourth) side of the frame with screws; this allows for the changing of a broken glass or reuse of the frame. Brass screws are advisable as they do not rust.

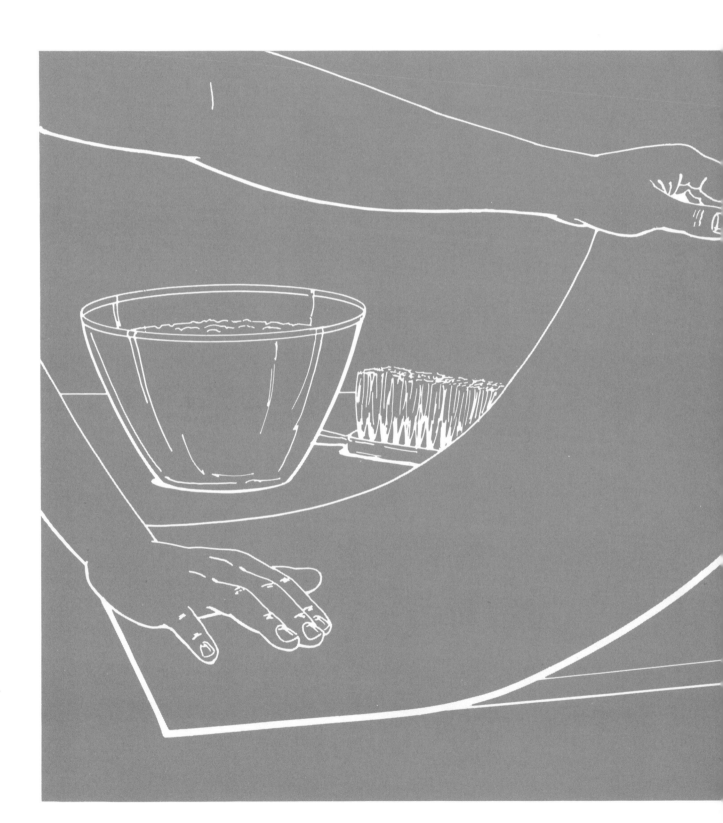

PART THREE

WHEAT
PASTE

MOUNTING

Mounting is the practice of attaching a work of art, a print, or a reproduction to a support for the purpose of making it flat or for reinforcement to ward off deterioration. There are two basic methods of mounting—wet mounting and dry mounting. For mounting reproductions or posters so that they may be hung without glass, I prefer the wet-mounting techniques. To affix the art to a support, I use the binding agent known as wheat paste. It has a neutral pH and is reversible, that is, you will be able to remove the art from the mounting board later. I use a basic cardboard product for the mounting board because of its affinity for the wheat paste. Upson board or chipboard work very well for this purpose and matboard or illustration board run a close second.

Once you have mounted the art and allowed the wheat paste to dry, you should spray on two coats of a light protective coating such as Krylon Crystal Clear spray. To hang the piece and prevent it from warping, I recommend a frame or a strainer; glass is not needed. I still have many inexpensive prints that I mounted more than thirty years ago that still look good. Often, I have used expensive frames to complement reproductions that may have cost only a few dollars. Although you can't argue that a reproduction can compare with an original piece of art, how many of us own a Vermeer or a Rembrandt? If properly framed, a good print can give years of enjoyment.

Another class of work suitable for mounting consists of damaged printed matter, such as maps or posters that have been folded or torn. Original art that has been done on inferior paper or has been handled poorly sometimes falls into this category. For example, drawings done on newsprint or oil paintings done on paper are destined to deteriorate if not mounted. Such pieces can be given an extended life by proper gluing to a longer lasting support. In some cases, these pieces may also require a certain amount of restoration after mounting. Broken ink patterns caused by folding can be fixed with watercolor or ink; and even sections of missing paper can be filled in with pastels when the mounted piece is

to be framed under glass. With some of these techniques, I have often made rumpled, crushed, folded, and torn pieces into perfectly acceptable subjects for framing.

When it comes to original art, mounting is a questionable solution. There are, of course, cases where mounting is the only way to protect the art and by necessity is the only solution; but, in general conservators and museums frown on mounting.

The techniques of wet mounting are simple but the products are numerous. There are a great many different brands of glue on the market, each claiming to have qualities the others do not. I have tried to stay out of this controversy and just give you the basic methods as I understand them. In addition to wet mounting and dry mounting, there is a class of adhesives available that are indeed "wet" but the liquid used is not water. These include such things as spray mounts and several kinds of contact cements. The solvents used in some of these can be dangerous to some art work. I think the best one I have used is called 77 made by the 3-M Company. You should be very careful about using it or any other spray adhesive on thin papers, however, as it will sometimes soak through and cause permanent discoloration of the paper. There are some sprays made especially for mounting photographs, and they seem to work fairly well; but I have often seen them come loose in time. The nice thing about spray adhesives is their speed and relative freedom from curl after mounting. On certain papers they will cause curling after spraying, but if you can get the paper down in a flat condition it usually will stay flat. This method is a good solution for mounting water-soluble pieces.

Contact cement is sometimes suggested for mounting art, but its use is questionable. (I have used it successfully to mount canvases; and perhaps, after all, it is really a hand-applied version of the spray adhesives.) It is usually applied to the back of the work and to the mounting board with a brush or roller and allowed to dry (about twenty minutes should be enough).

The piece must then be very carefully positioned and pressed into place. Once the contact is made there can be no moving the art—don't even try it! However, you can keep the surfaces apart with a "slip sheet," which is a piece of paper, until you have made the proper alignment. Then slip the paper out a tiny bit and adhere just the edge, after which you may pull the slip sheet out and press the entire piece in place. Remember, it's always a good idea to keep the surface of the work covered with a dry sheet of paper when you are pressing or rubbing. Contact cement holds very well and all the major brands are very much alike. Be warned, however, that there is a "water base" contact cement on the market. It is perfectly useless for art purposes, because in situations where you would be using contact cement, you are trying to avoid the use of water. As I have mentioned before, rubber cement should never be used unless you plan to photograph the work and throw it in the garbage; it simply has no place as a mounting medium.

When very large pieces of paper are mounted, you can reduce the weight by mounting on fabric instead of board. This is also true when the size exceeds the normal sizes available in mounting boards. Muslin is the most frequently used fabric for this purpose. It can be found in most fabric stores in its unbleached variety, and it's inexpensive. The other material I would suggest is called "sign cloth" and usually must be obtained from a supplier of sign painters' materials. This cloth has been primed with a white coating and is of a very fine weave (much finer than canvas). It is used to paint signs when large sizes are needed for more or less temporary use (not for permanent outdoor signs).

If you decide to mount on fabric, you must also make some sort of stretcher for the material. Ordinary canvas stretchers will suffice. If you are mounting on the sign cloth, a better glue than wheat paste is the vinyl paste used for cloth-backed wall coverings, such as Sanitas. The vinyl paste comes in plastic buckets in ready-to-use form. It makes a good bond and remains flexible should you want to roll up the finished piece.

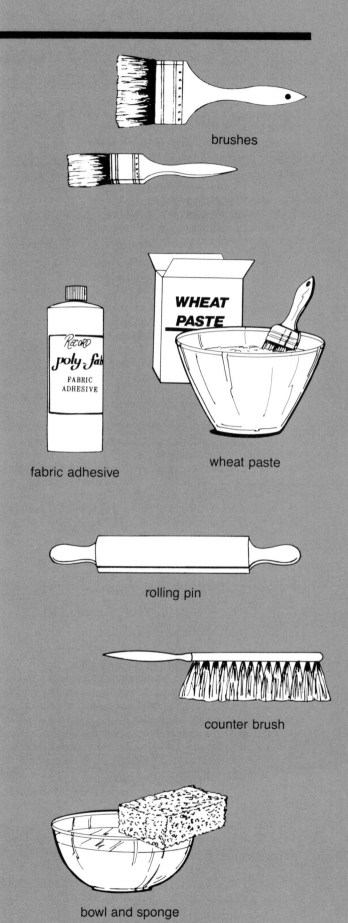

brushes

fabric adhesive

wheat paste

rolling pin

counter brush

bowl and sponge

WET MOUNTING

Wet mounting is the classic "wet mount" technique; it is the method used by most framers to mount reproductions and posters. I use it to mount drawings done on inferior paper, which is the example shown here. Wet mounting requires that the entire piece of art work be saturated with water, so this method is obviously not a good one for watercolors. Once you have determined that a piece can be wet mounted safely, cut the board at least 2″ (5.08 cm) larger than the piece in all directions; and if you are going to have a mat cut the board even larger. So don't make frames or mats until after you have done the mounting. You will also need two sheets of brown Kraft paper about the same size as the mounting boards.

You will need these things for mounting: a sponge, a container of water, a clean counter brush or some clean dry rags, and a bowl and brush for wheat paste. Wheat paste is the most basic of wallpaper pastes. You can use others, such as the cellulose paste used for fabric-backed vinyl coverings, but wheat paste is starch and is very close to the rice paste used to mount oriental scroll paintings and rice paper. Of course, rice paste will also work very well, since it is also a starch. I don't encourage the use of the new polyvinyl glues for fine art because it is questionable if the procedure can be reversed and, if needed, taken off the mount at a later date.

The drawing shown here is from a life drawing class and is done on newsprint with sanguine chalk. Because the drawing is so lovely, I decided to risk mounting it in order to preserve it. Otherwise, in a very few years, the paper will crumble because of its high acid content. Even with mounting, the paper will still turn amber with age, but the drawing itself will remain intact. To make sure that I don't smudge the drawing during the mounting process, I spray it with Krylon Crystal Clear spray. This step is particularly necessary with charcoal drawings, and I often use it for chalk and Conté crayon, too.

To begin the wet mounting process, cut two pieces of brown Kraft paper (ordinary wrapping paper) at least 2″ (5.08 cm) bigger than the drawing in all directions. Then, mix the wheat paste by shaking a little of it into a container of clear cold water. At the same time, constantly stir the mixture with the brush you will use to apply the paste. When you have reached the consistency of buttermilk (loose but slightly thick), the wheat paste should be ready. Let the paste stand a few minutes to develop the gluten.

Next, with the drawing lying face down on one of the sheets of brown paper, wet it from the back with clean water and a sponge. You should do this by patting rather than rubbing because the paper is easily torn when wet. To make sure the paper is thoroughly and uniformly wet, make a loose roll of the art and the brown paper, wetting both in the process. Then put the whole thing aside to soak for a few minutes. If you are mounting a group of pieces, you could put them into a plastic bag to keep them damp until you are ready to use them, much the way our mothers and grandmothers dampened clothes and put them away to soak until they were ready to iron.

When all is ready, unroll the first piece and check to see that it is thoroughly wet. Pick up any excess water with the sponge and apply the wheat paste to the back of the drawing with the brush. Go in all directions but try to avoid getting the paste on the face of the drawing. After applying the paste in a random pattern, go back to the far edge and draw the brush across in straight lines to distribute the paste and remove any puddles.

At this stage you have two choices. Either you can apply the mounting board to the back of the piece, or you can pick the paste-covered piece up and transfer it to the mounting board. I use the latter method when mounting large works such as posters. If you use the pick-up method, grasp the two top corners with the brown paper still in place (fold the edge of the brown paper under so you may grasp both easily) and hang the work on the board (which you have kept leaning against a wall or a piece of furniture).

Whichever method you use to apply the piece to the board, you now need to lay the work on the table and remove the brown paper, leaving the paste side up (you will have run over the edges of the piece when doing the pasting). Check to see that the mounted piece is lying flat; if it's not, pick up one corner and brush with the clean counter brush toward that corner to make the piece lie flat. Repeat this operation on all corners. If the paper is very delicate, cover it with a piece of dry brown paper when doing this step.

To make sure that contact has been made at every point of surface and that air bubbles or other flaws are gone, lay a sheet of brown paper (if you have not already used it in the smoothing down process) over the piece and apply pressure all over with a rolling pin or rub the surface well with a wad of dry rags. Now turn the piece over, keeping the dry brown paper in place to protect the front and apply the "countermount" to the back of the board. (The countermount is the first sheet of brown paper that by this time has dried out.) Re-wet the countermount with the sponge at least in its center section where the work had been. Then lay it aside and apply paste to the back of the mounting board on the area that describes where the piece is mounted on the other side. The area covered does not have to be exactly the same as the art, but should be in the general area. The idea is that the two papers pasted to the board will dry in opposition to each other, and thus will shrink evenly and prevent the board (and the piece) from any warping.

At this point lay the wet brown paper in place and smooth it with the brush. It is important to cut away any paper that is beyond the bounds of the paste. To trim the paper, use a razor blade and leave only the paper that is pasted on the board. The unpasted paper, especially where it sticks over the edge of the board, dries more rapidly than the pasted paper and will shrink unevenly, causing pulls and runs into the middle of the board.

Except for drying, this completes the wet-mounting process. To dry, let the finished pieces stand for a few minutes or even up to an hour. You will note that they will begin to curl or bow in at some point. When this happens, turn them over and let them bow the other way. (The bowing results from an uneven drying caused by varying exposures to air and heat.) Finally, place the mounted pieces flat on a table or the floor with a weight on top so that they may continue drying in a perfectly flat condition. A day or two in this condition will leave them with no tendency to curl. Now they may be trimmed to size and if they are to be framed without glass, as in the case of posters or reproductions, they can be sprayed with a fixative.

1 With the drawing lying face down on a sheet of brown paper, sponge clean water onto the back. Pat rather than rub so as not to abrade the paper.

2 Roll both drawing and brown paper into a loose roll and let soak.

3 Unroll and apply wheat paste to the back of the drawing.

4 Position the mounting board and lower it into place. Turn the board over and check to see that the paper is lying flat.

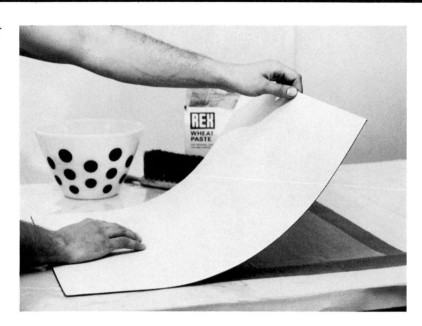

The mounted piece framed and matted.

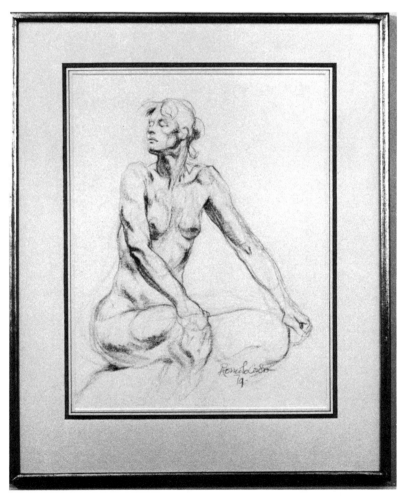

ALTERNATIVE METHODS

There are other methods of wet mounting. The one shown here is the example print from the French mat section; it is a mounting of a late-eighteenth century lithograph using the simple wet-mount process that requires no countermounting (because the print is not saturated with water). This particular method is suitable when the paper is of sufficient thickness and strength to retain a certain flatness when wetted with the paste. Size is also a factor here. I would not recommend doing large pieces this way. The further question of whether at some point in the future this is a piece you would want to remove from the mounting board should also be considered. As mentioned, I am not convinced that any of the white glue products are as easily removed as is wheat paste. However, there is a definite area for the use of this type of mounting; it still offers an alternative to dry mounting that is superior.

In this example I am using Polyfab; Jade Adhesive would do also, as would bookbinder's P.V.A. or Sobo. Whatever adhesive is used, dilute the glue a little with water (perhaps one quarter) to make it more brushable. Apply the paste to the back of the print with a brush or roller. Brush or roll in all directions to be sure of even distribution, then lay it out by brushing in only one direction.

Lay the paste-covered picture down on the mounting board, which in this case is ⅛″ (.32 cm) chipboard. Then, covering the piece with another paper, use a rolling pin or some other device to assure that good contact is made. Litho rollers are great but expensive; and those who have

them may not want them used in this way. A common rolling pin as used here will also suffice; or you can simply rub the surface with a wad of rags while covering the picture with a clean dry paper.

A variation of this alternative method of wet mounting is the same as the variant way of covering mats. Any of the glues mentioned can be used to coat the area on which the print lies. After the glue has dried, the print is positioned and ironed in place with a warm iron through a sheet of paper. This is a particularly good way to deal with delicate papers, such as rich paper or old semirotted papers with damaged areas.

Some of the pieces you may wish to mount will not be suitable for wet-mount processes. Silkscreen prints done with oil-based inks present a real problem. The printed parts of the paper expand at a slower rate than the part that is not printed. This makes for buckles, waves, and, in general, all sorts of problems. Watercolors, too, are difficult to do this way, although I have done some on heavy papers by applying the paste directly to the undampened picture or board. If the paper is rather wavy and doesn't want to lie down in a common plane, then you might try wetting it carefully from the back. It would be wise to fix it from the front with Krylon Crystal Clear beforehand. The back will expand, of course, causing the picture to arc in a cinemascope fashion toward the front. You can force it down anyway and put it under pressure to dry.

1 Apply polyvinyl glue directly to the back of the art. This method does not require pre-wetting the art.

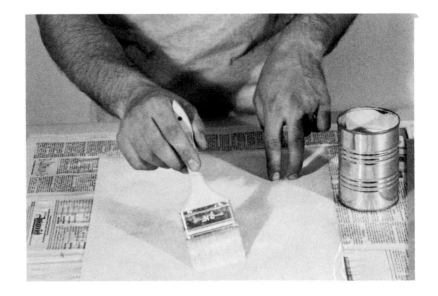

2 Place the art on the mounting board, protecting it with a clean sheet of paper. Use a rolling pin or other smoothing device, such as a heavy rag, to eliminate any air bubbles; make sure that contact is made over the entire surface.

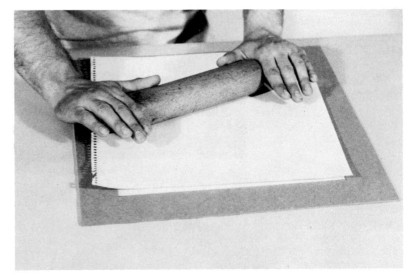

3 The mounting is completed at this stage. Because no water is used with this method, countermounting is not necessary. Unlike the wheat paste used in wet mounting, the polyvinyl glue will prevent the art from curling.

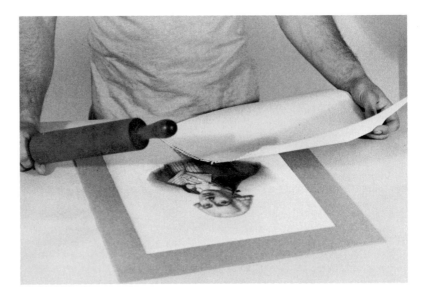

DRY MOUNTING

The people who make dry-mounting machines claim that dry mounting is a wonderful way to mount works of art. But it is also possible to do dry mounting without the use of special machines. The Seal brand makes a decent dry-mount tissue that holds well when applied with a warm iron. However, most of the other dry-mount tissues are questionable. If they don't work, the manufacturers will undoubtedly say that the temperature of your iron wasn't right—and that indeed may be true. I am only trying to give you a method that will not end in disappointment. In general, if you are mounting photographs under 16″ × 20″ (40.6 × 50.8 cm), the dry-mount press will probably give satisfactory results with any of the standard tissues; over that size I recommend Seal brand. But if you are mounting art prints, posters, or reproductions, I don't recommend dry mounting at all. The reason is that it is truly irreversible. Without tremendous effort, you can't remove the piece and try another method. To begin with, most dry-mount presses don't exceed 24″ × 30″ (60.9 × 76.2 cm). This means that if you are mounting a larger piece, you would have to place it in the press two or three times from various sides. This never works. It *seems*

to work for a while, but eventually air bubbles or rolls form on the surface where the mounting has not held. Even more unfortunate is the fact that most dry-mount systems, even if you are able to unmount the pieces, leave a residue on the paper. Then, the only real alternative you have is to redo the same process, hoping it will hold the second time around.

To conclude, I repeat my warning about mounting in general—don't do it unless you absolutely need to. Although both matting and framing won't protect your art from atmospheric conditions, when these conditions, such as extreme humidity, go back to normal, a certain waviness in the paper will return to its original flat condition. For me this is as natural as molting birds or shedding dogs. But I have experienced frame shops where every piece framed has also been mounted so that the whole thing comes out looking very slick and superfinished. This has a certain mass appeal; it seems to fit our refrigerator, television, automobile kind of look in the late-twentieth century. So if you must mount, follow correct procedure and be very careful and very neat; and for wet mounts, make sure to allow plenty of drying time before removing from the press.

GLOSSARY

alkyd base paint—a class of oil paints based on alkyd resins, ordinarily used for interior decoration, for example, on walls. For framing purposes the basic flat white is usually tinted by adding ordinary artist's oil colors.

antiquing—a term sometimes used to describe a toning process that gives the finish of a frame a softer, hence older look. It is the final stage in the development of a patina on the finish.

appliqué—ornamentation accomplished by applying cutout shapes or designs, sometimes in several layers, to a surface. The word usually refers to fabric sewed onto other fabric, but in picture framing it means any thin pieces or cutout shapes that are glued onto a larger surface.

asphaltum varnish—an intensely black varnish containing asphalt. It is used in this book as an additive to japan colors for backing gold leaf gilding on glass. It has many other uses such as the ground for etching on a metal plate.

awl—a tool resembling a screwdriver except that it has a pointed end (like an ice pick). One of its uses is to start the hole for a small screw or screw eye.

backing piece—a stiff material used to support the artwork in the frame and help to keep it close against the glass. Most backing pieces are made of corrugated cardboard, chipboard or foamcore. They should be the same size as the mat and, if it is a folder mat, be placed immediately behind it.

backsaw—the kind of saw used in a steel miter box. It has a straight blade with fine teeth, and its top edge is stiffened with a heavier piece of steel forming a "back," which rests in the supports of the miter box and keeps the saw from touching the metal of the table part of the box.

Bainbridge matboard—the most popular and widespread brand of matboard on the market. This company has, for many years, established the standards and the trends for this product. There are others; but they always try to imitate or follow the Bainbridge lead. You can safely use the Bainbridge line as a point of reference.

benzine—a volatile solvent derived from petroleum, which is more or less equal to mineral spirits. Benzene is another matter and is not safe to use. Of course no solvents are perfectly safe to use, but benzine is probably as safe as turpentine.

beveled edge—an edge tapered at an angle to make a more gradual transition between an upper and a lower surface. The beveled edge of a mat inclines about 60°. The beveled edge of a straight-edge is more gradual, causing it to be quite wide. The bevel of a straight-edge does not go all the way to the bottom surface (as does that of a mat) but leaves a small, vertical blunt edge so that it will be less liable to damage and not so knifelike.

bevels—in reference to molding shapes, those designs created by one or more straight cuts made at an angle to the right-angle condition of the rabbet, thus creating a sloping face or back or both. A bevel is also a tool, a sort of adjustable square used to find or copy and transfer the angle of a beveled surface or line.

binding agent—a substance such as varnish or boiled linseed oil that is added to a toning mixture to cause it to adhere firmly to the surface to which it is applied. Turpentine and boiled oil or varnish constitute the vehicle of the toning solution, which carries the pigment in suspension. After application the turpentine evaporates, leaving the pigment bound to the surface by the binding agent.

bole—a friable clay of a reddish brown color close to burnt sienna in tone. It has long been the favorite base for the water-gilding size used to lay real gold leaf on a gesso ground. The bole is mixed with rabbit-skin glue and water.

bookbinder's P.V.A.—polyvinyl adhesive used in the manufacture and repair of books. In the framing process, it is used to stick various covering materials to mats and for some kinds of mounting.

bowing—warping or curving out of the flat condition. A frequent problem with mounted pieces, it is dealt with by countermounting, gluing a piece of paper to the back of the mounting board so that the mounted piece and the paper dry at the same time, pulling in opposition to each other, hence keeping the board flat.

box nails—one of the basic varieties of nails. They are thinner than common nails but not so thin as finishing nails. They have rather large, thin heads and are frequently used to assemble boxes. Box nails have little use in framing.

box-style frame—"the" basic picture frame. It is simply a strip of molding, the profile of which forms a vertical rectangle with the rabbet cut into its side. The face is narrower than the back or depth. A typical box molding might be one with a ¾" face and a 2" depth with the rabbet cut ¼" down from the face. When a simple rectilinear molding is turned and has its rabbet cut so that it must be used in a horizontal position, it is known as a flat. See also flat.

brads, wire brads—the small nails used to join small frames and to fasten the backings to frames of all sizes. They are sold by the length and the gauge of the wire from which they are cut. The larger the number the smaller the diameter of the wire. Typical sizes used for framing are ¾ × 18, 1 × 18, 1 × 16, and 1¼ × 16.

butt joining—placing one piece of wood against another and connecting them with nails and glue or other fasteners.

casein paint—a water-based paint widely used by scenic painters in the theater. It is made from pigments bound by casein, the nonbutterfat solids of milk. The color range is roughly the same as for oil colors, and casein colors are sold in cans like house paints. (There are artist's casein colors also, which are sold in tubes, but these are not the caseins mentioned in this book.) They come in paste form and must be thinned with water to usable consistency. They dry rapidly and become semiwaterproof, which means that brushes must be washed as soon as possible after use.

chipboard—the gray pulpboard or cardboard used for backing pads of paper. It is not to be confused with particle board or flake board, which are builders' supplies made from chips or particles of wood.

clay size—the adhesive agent used to attach real gold leaf to a gessoed surface. See also Bole.

claw hammer—the most common type of hammer for general use. It has two curving projections on the head, which are used to extract nails. The smaller hammers weighing ten to fourteen ounces will be most useful for framing.

colored-bevel technique—the method for applying watercolor or ink to the bevel of a cut mat to create a more dramatic effect by emphasizing some color in the artwork. The manner of holding the brush and applying the color are demonstrated in the matting section. Sometimes pastels are used for this purpose. If so, they must be fixed to prevent smudging.

colonial molding—one of the most widely used moldings for picture framing. It is available in a number of sizes and is finished in a variety of ways to achieve widely varying effects. See the French mat section for the profile and its typical use.

combination square—a small carpenter's square consisting of a steel 1′ ruler and a sliding headpiece, which can be used to give either 90° or 45° readings. The 90° side can be set and used like a marking gauge. Some versions also have a centering device for circles.

common nails—the type of nails used for general carpentry, forms for concrete, and rough work. They have rather thick shafts topped with broad heads. They are not used in conditions where it is desired to "set" the heads into the wood and putty the holes. Such nails are called finishing nails and are much thinner with small, ball-like heads. Both kinds of nails have their size stated the same way, by the "penny." Penny size is indicated by the length in numerals followed by the English penny sign as 4d, 6d, 8d, 10d, and so on. These sizes represent 1½″, 2″, 2½″, and 3″ in length. The nails are sold by the pound.

countermount—in the mounting process, a piece of paper attached to the back of the mounting board by the same method used to attach the artwork to the front and done immediately afterward to insure that the board remains in a flat condition. See also bowing.

cove—a curved recess or a concave groove in a molding, such as the cove in colonial molding. See also the molding chart.

covered mat—an ordinary paperboard mat with cloth or paper attached to its surface to create a particular effect. See the oval mat section for an example covered with moleskin.

crown molding—one of the standard household moldings available in lumberyards. It can be combined with other shapes to make attractive picture-frame moldings.

dead-end ruler—any rule or ruler than starts from the very end of the piece of material from which it is made, thus enabling you to make measurements by abutting the end of the ruler against something. Many rulers (such as an architect's scale) start from a mark made some distance from the end.

deckle—the natural uneven edge on handmade paper or an edge torn to simulate it. Tearing wet paper against a saw or straightedge is one way to make a deckle edge.

Dexter cutter—a commonly available mat-cutting device. It is a metal tool holding a blade at an angle. It can be slid along a straightedge to make the beveled cut for a mat opening. There are a number of other very similar cutters on the market.

diagonals, or dykes—the common names of the electrician's diagonal wire cutters, similar to pliers but with cutting edges the full length of the blades.

distressing—the practice of making a frame (or sometimes furniture) look old or worn and damaged. It is not meant to make "fake" antiques so much as it is meant to create softer, more mellow effects.

double-thick matboard—matboard that is twice the thickness of the standard.

drop-on technique—a method of matting in which the artwork is simply laid on top of a matboard or other backing and held in place by linen hinges or other attachment so that it "floats" rather than having its edges covered by the window of a mat. The technique is sometimes used in combination with an actual cut mat as in the example for a linen-covered mat.

dry-mount—a technique used principally to mount photographs by attaching them to a board with dry-mount tissue and heat. The full system uses a dry-mount press. The piece is backed with dry-mount tissue held in place by "tacking" with a small tacking iron and is positioned on the board and placed in the dry-mount press. The press is closed for a timed interval to suit the type of tissue being used. The heat fuses the tissue to both the picture and the backing.

easel back—an arrangement attached to the back of a picture frame to cause it to stand on a table or other flat surface. It is usually a permanent and integral part of the frame. See the section on easel back.

emulsion-coated—covered by a film of gelatin or other suspension agent containing the dispersed particles of silver salts or other light-sensitive chemicals held in suspension.

engraving—an art printing process in which lines and images are cut with tools into metal plates or wood blocks, which are then inked, wiped off, and printed. The ink remaining in the grooves makes the design. Paper money is an example of fine engraving. It is sometimes confused with etching, a process in which the lines or images are usually eaten into the plate by acid. Both these intaglio processes are distinguished from relief printing, in which lines are made on a wood or linoleum block by removing the background materials. Ink is applied to the raised parts of the block, which, when the block is printed, make the design.

escutcheon pins—small, dome-headed brass nails used to fasten escutcheons, which are decorative additions to furniture such as keyhole covers or rosettes at the base of handles, often made of brass but sometimes of wood.

etching—an intaglio printing process in which the lines are scratched through a protective coating on a metal plate, which is then immersed in acid. The acid "bites" the image into the metal surface, which is then inked, wiped, and printed. See also Engraving.

feather spline—a small sliver of hardwood inserted across the corner of a mitered picture frame to strengthen it. Sometimes several splines are used in one joint. They can also be quite decorative if done in a wood other than the wood of the frame and given a natural finish.

finishing nails—the second most commonly used nails. They are relatively thin and have small heads. See also Common nails.

GLOSSARY

fitch—a style of artist's brush having medium-length bristles and tied in a somewhat rounded flat shape resembling a straw broom. These brushes usually have long handles and are very good for applying decorative finishes. They are well adapted to a whisking action and dry-brush effects.

fitting—the assembly process in framing. After the frame has been cut and finished, the fitting process begins; it includes cutting the glass, cutting the mat and backing, and assembling all the parts into a finished piece. People who do this operation professionally are known as fitters.

flat, or flat-style frame—a molding of rectilinear profile with a rabbet cut so that it will be used in a horizontal position. A typical flat might be ¾″ thick by 3″ wide and have a rabbet cut in ³⁄₁₆″ down from the front, or face. It would then present a sort of matlike effect. Flats can be small or large, and they can be used in combination with other moldings to create styles such as the railroad or center-panel. What distinguishes them as flats is their being parallel to the wall; in other words, they are used in a horizontal position when the molding is seen in cross section.

Fletcher cutter—a glass cutter of the steel wheel variety; the number 2 with a steel ball at the end of the handle is recommended.

floating effect—floating frames in which the rabbet, if there is one, is used in reverse; that is, the picture is placed in from the front rather than from the back. This means that the edge of the picture is not covered. Many frames of this type have a small reveal next to the painting (say ¼″ down and ¼″ over) before adding a frame that comes flush or in front of the face of the picture. This frame normally does not receive glass and so is suitable for canvas and panels.

fly-specking—the practice of applying small dark dots of paint to the finish of a frame to resemble the natural ones left there by flies. (Flies love to make deposits on gold or shiny surfaces.) The process is accomplished by flicking paint from a toothbrush or other stiff-bristled brush, knocking it on the edge of a stick to create a spattering.

folder mat—the basic paperboard mat or covered mat hinged together with a sheet of plain matboard or museum board of the same size. The hinging is usually done with linen tape. The artwork is then positioned in the window of the mat and held in place by hinging it to the backing board.

French mat—the most antique decorative style of matting in common use. The mats have ruled lines surrounding the window. There are typically two to ten lines of varying interval and weight. Many times the space between two of the lines is filled with a wash of watercolor or other decorative effect; and usually at least one of the lines is gold.

fresco colors—a term often applied to casein paints, which are actually not used to paint frescoes. They are excellent, quick-drying paints that are very popular with theatrical scenic painters and display artists.

gas pliers—the most common type of pliers. They have slip jaws that can accommodate larger objects than their normal grip.

German method—a practice of adding a second piece of glass to a framed and matted piece. It is placed behind the folder mat and is taped together with the front piece to create a totally sealed sandwich, which is then held in the frame with backing and nailing.

gesso—a mixture of whiting and animal glue or gelatin. It must be applied warm after liquifying it in a double boiler. This is the gesso traditionally used by artists, gilders, and framers. There is also gesso made with plaster and glue and used to do bas-relief decoration on ceilings and walls. The manufacturers of acrylic paints have chosen to mislabel their basic white paint "gesso," leading to a great deal of confusion since the product is not similar to, or desirable as a substitute for, real gesso.

gilded finish—any surface to which a metallic appearance has been applied. In this book the term is used exclusively to mean leafing with one of the metal leaf products or real gold.

gilder's tip—a particular kind of brush especially made for the laying of gold leaf. It has 2″ bristles assembled in a 3″ row. The bristles are very soft, like camel hair or ox hair, or even finer. They are held in a cardboard handle. The brush is passed lightly across the gilder's hair, a woolen garment, or a dog. This action produces static and a slight oiliness in the bristles so they will attract and hold the leaf. The leaf is picked up on the side of the brush, transported to the desired position, and then laid on the matured size.

glass mat—a style of matting in which the mat is literally applied to the surface of the glass. Usually gold and black, this style has been in favor for many years for such subjects as English hunting prints. The frames are often of colonial molding with various gilded treatments. The mat itself is produced by masking out lines or spaces. The glass left exposed is painted with black japan color or black enamel. The gold leaf is laid in the lines, which have received gelatin size.

glazier—a person who cuts and fits glass, especially for windows. A glazier's shop is the source for glass for your frames. The glazier will cut it to size for you, or you can buy larger pieces and cut them yourself.

glazing—the craft of the glazier, one who cuts and fits glass. It is also the art of interior decoration that concerns itself with shading or antiquing walls and other surfaces. A related meaning is the process of toning frames.

gouache—a water-based paint containing Chinese white, which makes it opaque. It is often used in combination with transparent watercolor and even pastel.

gold leaf—in the strictest sense is 22 karat gold pounded to very, very thin sheets or leaves. These sheets are attached to various surfaces by means of several different kinds of size, or adhesive. In a wider sense the term also applies to the use of metal leaf as a substitute for real gold. Many frames that are advertised as gold leaf are indeed "leafed" but are not gold. See also Metal leaf.

grass cloth—a kind of paper-backed, semiwoven, grass-textured "cloth" most often used as a wall covering. Sometimes one sees it on lamp-shades. It is very often used to give an oriental effect.

grozing—the practice of "chewing" away at the edge of a piece of glass with the teeth of a pair of pliers. By this method the glass can be brought into line or made to match another piece. There are special pliers for this process, but it can be performed with ordinary gas pliers or electrician's pliers.

grommet—a reinforcement for a hole or opening in a material that is likely to tear. Grommets are often made of brass or other metal. They can be quite simply attached with a small device available in any hardware store.

high rag content—paper that is made chiefly from linen or cotton fibers rather than from wood pulp, which is highly acid. High rag content usually indicates a neutral pH.

hinge—a small piece of linen tape or other neutral material such as mulberry paper that is folded in half and glued to the artwork and the backing or sometimes is not folded but laid across the top edge of the art and onto the backing. The term also applies to a strip of tape used to join the mat to a backing piece of board to create a folder mat.

horizontal mat—a mat having a window opening wider than it is high. A horizontal mat is normally cut to even proportions all around or with very little increase in the bottom edge (such as ¼″) to account for visual drop. Vertical mats usually are at least ½″ wider at the bottom.

illustration board—a kind of paperboard that is slightly thicker than matboard and has dark layers in the interior, which makes it unsuitable for mats. It is surfaced with a somewhat toothed white paper suitable for a variety of painting techniques. It receives watercolor and gouache and many drawing media as well. It is the favorite working surface for most graphic artists.

inlay mat—a mat made somewhat in the manner of the French mat but in which the lines and borders are actually "let in" pieces of matboard. These mats can only be made by mat-cutting machines. The tolerances are too close for hand-cut mats.

Jade Adhesive—brand name for bookbinder's polyvinyl adhesive.

japan—a quick-drying varnish. The term refers to lacquer made from the resin of a tree known as "the oriental tree," or *Rhus vernicifera,* which has been used for centuries for Chinese and Japanese lacquer work. The term is also used for a variety of natural-resin varnishes with added color, which Europeans use in an effort to duplicate oriental lacquer. The technique of applying japan is called japanning.

japan colors—a modern term for quick-drying, lusterless paints mixed with turpentine or lacquer thinner used by sign painters and framers.

japan dryer—the basic unthickened resin obtained from the oriental lac tree. This resin, when allowed to thicken, becomes what is known as japan lac. This is the *vehicle* for japan colors. When added to boiled linseed oil it becomes gold size (quick or slow, according to how much is added.) See also Shellac.

japan gold-size—the standard oil-gilding medium. It comes in two varieties, quick and slow; the first is used when the amount of gilding to be done is relatively small, the second when the job is large. The size is not applied until the surface has been brought to the stage of applying a final varnish. Porous materials must first be primed and sealed. After painting a thin uniform layer of the size (used straight from the can without thinning), wait the appropriate time before testing to see if the size is ready to receive the leaf. The quick size matures in one to three hours, the slow in ten to thirteen. Touch the knuckle of your middle finger to the size; it is ready if it comes away with a "ticking" sound.

joining—putting together the mitered pieces of molding to form a frame.

joining hammer—a small to medium claw hammer used to nail the corners of a picture frame.

jute canvas—a brown canvas of coarse texture made of the same fibers to make burlap. It is sold in art supply stores as a support for paintings.

Kraft paper—the common brown wrapping paper used by most businesses. It comes in rolls and is sold by weight and width in inches.

Krylon Crystal Clear spray—a pressurized spray can of water-clear acrylic lacquer. It makes an excellent fixative and sealant. It is waterproof and very quick drying. Use only with adequate ventilation.

lap-jointed—joined by means of half-lapping, cutting away half the material from each side of two overlapping members so that they remain in one plane. This is the most frequently used joint in all woodworking. It is strong and self-squaring.

layered mat—a double or triple mat, a mat made up of several pieces of matboard one on top of the other.

"laying it out"—after paint or paste has been randomly brushed on a surface in all directions, the smoothing or unifying process of dragging the brush back and forth across the surface in one direction.

layout—in the sense of this book, the drawing of the window opening for a mat or the penciling in of the lines on a French mat.

leafing—the process of covering a surface with metallic leaf (thin foil), usually gold metal leaf or aluminum leaf but sometimes real gold or silver. There are several other kinds of leaf such as variegated, copper, yellow gold, and palladium.

liner—an inner frame used with a usually larger outer frame for a painting. Liners are often flat but sometimes beveled at the front edge.

litho roller—a brayer, or large hand-held roller, for applying ink to a lithographic stone for printing. It is usually made of gelatin or synthetic rubber.

lithograph—a print made by a surface printing process dependent on the rejection of oil and water or some similar attraction-and-repulsion system. The classic type is the stone lithograph, in which the image is made on a smooth piece of fine limestone by drawing with a lithographic crayon or painting with tusche. The stone is then soaked with water and inked with an oil-based ink, which is attracted to the oily surface of the image but repelled by the wet stone. Paper is put in place and pressure is applied by running it through a press to transfer the ink to the paper.

marking block—a rectangular bar of hardwood about 2 or 2½′ long and perhaps 3″ wide by 2″ high. It should be very straight and heavy; rock maple is good. It is used as point of reference for the edge of the mat and the end of the ruler when you need to abut something to make marks for cutting or drawing. It also functions as a weight and is a useful addition to your work space.

marking gauge—a standard carpenter's tool usually made of wood and brass; but there are other metal versions. It has a movable block riding on an arm marked with a scale. The block is held in a desired position by a thumbscrew, and the mark is made by a steel point or pencil lead at the end of the arm. It is used to draw a line parallel to an edge.

matboard—a type of paperboard made especially for matting pictures. It is sold in art supply stores and is available in a wide variety of colors. The standard size is 30″ or 32″ × 40″; but there is 40″ × 60″ also in some colors, and whites are available in several other sizes.

mat cutter—a device used to cut windows in mats. There are whole setups with rails and measuring boards, but the only ones discussed in this book are of the hand-held block variety, which hold a blade at an angle and are pushed along a standard straightedge.

metal leaf—composition leaf, or imitation gold. It comes in between sheets of tissue in book form. The leaves are 5″ × 5″ and there are twenty-five in a book. Twenty books constitute a pack, or five hundred leaves. It can be purchased by the book or by the pack. It is also available in loose form without the tissues, and it comes in a box of five hundred leaves.

miter—the angle cut marking the halfway point of the crossing of two pieces of molding of equal width; hence the miter cut most frequently used is a 45° making up half of the 90° corner of a conventional frame.

miter box—an arrangement of two planes producing a right angle into which the molding can be pressed while cutting it with the miter saw, which is held by a special arrangement of vertical posts in the position of any desired angle. The best miter boxes are the steel variety, as shown in this book; the wooden ones used to cut interior trim moldings don't give very long service.

miter saw—the type of backsaw usually used with a miter box. See Backsaw.

miter joint—the equally divided joint at the corner of a picture frame. The two angled cuts must together make up the full angle of the corner, which is usually 90°.

molding—a strip of wood provided with a rabbet to receive the glass, mat, backing, or whatever other contents the frame is to hold. The strip may be simple in profile or may be made ornamental by the addition of grooves or beveled cuts. In fact a simple strip of wood *without* a rabbet is also referred to as molding; but we are dealing here with framing.

moleskin—a kind of short-napped velveteen that makes a good mat covering.

mounting—the attaching of a piece of artwork to a support for the purpose of extending its life or bracing it to show at better advantage. Mounting usually means gluing the entire surface of the back of the art to a board or other support such as a stretched canvas.

mulberry paper hinges—mounting hinges made of paper made from the bark of the paper mulberry tree and coated with an acid-free glue.

museum board—100 percent rag matboard. It has a uniform color throughout and is acid free. It is sometimes lumped together with conservator's matboard, which is not 100 percent rag but has a neutral pH.

nailing edge—a bar of hardwood attached to the edge of a work table with two small "C" clamps for the purpose of backing the edge of a frame into which you are driving nails during the fitting or assembly process.

"nailing on the mat"—piercing the corrugated backing and then pushing the wire brad down flat so that when the nail is driven in, it will be sliding on the back of the mat.

natural pongee—fine, sheer fabric woven from the unbleached thread of raw silk.

newsprint—the white pulp paper on which newspapers are printed. It has high acid content and is quick to deteriorate, but artists love it because it is cheap and it has a natural tooth that receives the chalk and charcoal very well. It is used as a basic drawing pad in most schools and even by professionals.

no-mat mat—an effect created by framing an artwork on paper sandwiched between two glass panels in a frame so as to leave a "mat" area around the work. Thus the wall color becomes the mat color.

nonporous—without absorbent qualities. Nonporous materials generally have to be sealed in order to receive their final finish.

oil gilding—the most common method for applying leafed finishes. For these gold size is used (japan gold-size).

O'Keeffe molding—the rounded, roll-back style of molding made famous by the painter Georgia O'Keeffe, who used it to frame her pictures.

oval mat—a mat with an oval opening but usually a rectangular circumference. Sometimes, when an oval frame is used, the oval mat is cut to fit.

overmat—the mat that is applied on top of an undermat to create a multiple-layered effect such as the double mat or triple mat.

palladium leaf—a leaf similar to gold leaf made from a rare metal in the platinum family. A lustrous warm silver color, it is more satisfactory for a silver look than silver itself because it doesn't tarnish.

particle-board—generic term for panels made of sawdust or wood chips.

passe-partout—a kind of "framing" in which no actual frame is used. The matted artwork is placed together with glass and backing in a sandwich condition and the edges are bound with tape (usually white linen). The backing is pierced with two holes through which the prongs of the passe-partout rings are passed. Wire is placed between the rings for hanging.

pebbled matboard—matboard whose surface has been embossed to give a bumpy, textured look, rather like leatherette, and also to add stiffness.

Poly-fab—a polyvinyl glue whose name suggests its function—it is good for gluing down all kinds of fabrics. It is also useful as a mounting adhesive.

pH—a chemistry symbol used to express the activity of the hydrogen atom in relation to the acidity of a particular material. It expresses the relative alkaline or acid condition on a scale of 0 to 14, 7 representing neutrality.

polyvinyl adhesive (P.V.A.)—the basic "white" glue which is used to glue everything. It has many variations, which are discussed in some sections of the text.

quick size—adhesive used in gold leafing that matures to a tacky state in one to three hours; as opposed to slow size, which sets in ten to thirteen hours.

rabbet—the L-shaped groove at the inner edge of a picture frame, which receives the contents of the frame.

ragboard—another name for museum board.

Roman gold—a traditional name for gold finishes of a rich reddish hue. It is produced on metal-leafed surfaces by toning with a lot of burnt sienna or Venetian red added to the toner.

rottenstone—a very finely powdered limestone with an abrasive quality. It is used as a polishing agent, but picture frames use it as imitation dust, to soften toned effects.

Sanitas—a brand name for a vinyl, cloth-backed wall covering, usually used in kitchens or bathrooms.

sash brush—a round paintbrush about 1¼″ in diameter with medium-length bristles. It is designed for painting window sashes, but I like it for painting with casein, for antique white, and for stippling toned finishes.

score—the scratch made on the surface of a sheet of glass by the steel wheel of a glass cutter.

Seal—brand name for a particular kind of dry-mount tissue I think the best kind for use without a press.

section frame—the aluminum frame that is offered in its sectional pieces in most art supply stores. It is available in gold and silver as well as several colors. The pieces are sold in plastic envelopes or boxes with two pieces to a package. They come in equal inches but can be sawed to fit other sizes. They are easily assembled using screwdrivers or in some instances hex wrenches (which are furnished with the kit).

shantung—a silk fabric made from a coarsely twisted thread so that it exhibits an uneven texture. The thread has enlarged sections at frequent intervals. It makes interesting mat covering, especially in natural or raw color. It is frequently used to cover lampshades.

shellac—a solution prepared from the secretion of the lac bug. It is naturally amber (orange) in color but is usually bleached white. It is dissolved in alcohol and is used as a sealant, filler, and separator.

short-napped covering—velveteen or moleskin.

sign cloth—a thin, fine-weave cotton canvas already sized and primed white, used chiefly by sign painters to execute large interior or temporary signs and banners.

slow size—See Quick size.

Sobo—a brand name for polyvinyl white glue. It has additives that cause it to remain very flexible, similar to bookbinder's P.V.A.

spacer—a strip of wood or sometimes cardboard used to keep the contents of a frame from touching the glass.

spirit level—a device used in construction and elsewhere to maintain true horizontal and vertical relationships. It operates on the principle of a bubble trapped in a liquid inside a slightly curved tube. When the bubble finds the center of the tube, the surface on which the level is resting has reached a true horizontal or vertical.

spray mount—a kind of rubberized adhesive available in aerosol cans. It is widely used to mount photographs and small artwork. There are many variations of this product so that the label must be read carefully. I have found the most satisfactory one for all-round purposes is the 3M-77 brand.

Spackle—a product made from high-quality plaster of paris and glue along with a retarder. It comes in powdered form and can be mixed with water to any desired consistency. Spackle is a brand name and is made only by the Muralo Company. Other companies make variations called spackling compounds, but none are as good as the original.

stain—coloring used to change the appearance of wood. There are oil stains and water stains and alcohol stains, but for framing purposes you can make a very satisfactory stain by simply diluting oil color with turpentine.

stippling—the action of pouncing a surface with the ends of a brush. For stippling a toned frame a large fluffy brush is best. The stippling action should serve to distribute the color into a uniform glaze.

straight-edge—a ruler or a plain strip of metal at least 3′ long. The best ones are beveled on one edge to make them thinner so that the knife, when held on an angle and guided along the edge, will be closer to the line.

strainer, or retainer—a flat wood frame usually ⅝″ to ¾″ thick × 1½″ to 2″ wide. In larger sizes it will have a cross brace. The joints are best made as lap-joints. Its purpose is to be inserted in the back of a picture frame to reinforce and carry the weight of the glass and contents. The hanging system is attached to this frame so that the actual frame has no stress on its mitered corners.

swan molding—a very popular molding profile with a rounded top, or face, and a gentle roll back and an up turn at the back. Its profile is somewhat reminiscent of the profile of a swan.

tack—to attach in a few spots, as in dry-mounting to position the piece before placing it in the press. Tacks are small nails of a style little used in picture framing; carpet tacks are useful and good for the stretching of canvas; but for framing wire brads are used.

tack hammer—an upholsterer's tool widely used by framers. It is a small hammer with a curved head (the best ones at least) and a face about the size of a nickle. I usually grind the side that will be on the bottom when nailing the brads into the backing to a flat surface, thus allowing more of the face for striking the brad. Its ears, or split end (which is for pulling webbing), are magnetic and useful for recovering brads.

tickled finish—any finish that has been highly worked with many layers of tonings and spattering or texturing.

toning—the application of a glaze over a basic finish to give depth and richness. The undercoat is usually isolated with shellac and the toning mixture, made of oil or japan color and turpentine, is mixed with a little boiled linseed oil or varnish for better bonding.

tungsten carbide cutter—a glass cutter with the wheel made of very hard carbide steel. It is much longer lasting than a regular steel wheel.

Upson board—a brand name for a builder's cardboard available in lumberyards in 4′ × 8′ sheets.

GLOSSARY

undermat—the bottom mat in instances where there are two or more layers, as in double or triple matting.

vignetted—an effect widely used in photography in which the image is printed in such a way that the edges fade and disappear into the tone of the paper, leaving a more or less oval shape. The term is also used in printing to indicate small decorations or pictures at the beginning or end of chapters, for instance. The characteristic vignette is borderless.

vertical mat—a mat turned so that its greater dimension is up and down.

vise—a tool attached to a workbench and used to clamp or hold a piece of work.

visual drop—an optical effect that causes low horizontal elements to seem smaller than they would be if they were turned in a vertical position. This effect can be compensated for by increasing the bottom side of a mat.

wash—a broad area covered by a continuous tone of watercolor, gouache, or ink.

water gilding—the form of gold leafing in which clay size is used over a gesso ground. This method is used for real gold and especially when it is intended to burnish it to a high luster. Gold laid on oil size cannot be burnished.

water putty—a product made for filling holes in wood. It is basically plaster of paris with glue and color added. It is mixed with water and used immediately, as it sets very rapidly.

wet-mount—the technique of gluing artwork to a support with water-based adhesives.

wheat paste—wallpaper adhesive made from wheat flour mixed with cold water to a consistency of cream. It is used for wet-mounting.

whetstone—a smooth, flat stone used for sharpening knives or tools.

window—the opening in a mat.

wire brads—small nails, similar to finishing nails, used for framing.

wood putty—see Water putty.

wood cut—a print made from a wood block bearing an image cut in relief. The lines are raised and the background cut away.

INDEX

INDEX